RACHEL VOGELEISEN

IN THEIR
OWN WORDS

WOMEN WHO SERVED IN WORLD WAR II

Mereo Books

1A The Wool Market Dyer Street Cirencester Gloucestershire GL7 2PR
An imprint of Memoirs Publishing www.mereobooks.com

First published in Great Britain in 2015
by Mereo Books, an imprint of Memoirs Publishing

The address for Memoirs Publishing Group Limited can be found at www.memoirspublishing.com

The Memoirs Publishing Group Ltd Reg. No. 7834348

The Memoirs Publishing Group supports both The Forest Stewardship Council® (FSC®) and the
PEFC® leading international forest-certification organisations. Our books carrying both the FSC
label and the PEFC® and are printed on FSC®-certified paper. FSC® is the only
forest-certification scheme supported by the leading environmental organisations including
Greenpeace. Our paper procurement policy can be found at
www.memoirspublishing.com/environment

Design: Ray Lipscombe

Typeset in 9/14pt Bembo
by Wiltshire Associates Publisher Services Ltd. Printed and bound in Great Britain by
Printondemand-Worldwide, Peterborough PE2 6XD

LAND ARMY GIRLS

CONTENTS

Thank you note
Foreword

A WORD ABOUT THE SERVICES

WOMEN WHO SERVED

THANK YOU

This book is dedicated to the people who have taught me history with real passion and shared their experiences of the Second World War: M. Acker, my first history teacher at the *collège* in Benfeld; Mrs Fabre at the Lycée Notre Dame des Mineurs in Strasbourg; my grandfather, René Hornung, who told me about his campaign in Russia while we were walking along the road up to the village of Biguglia in Corsica; and Suzo (Pascal) Terribile, whose story I have been tracking down for the last fifteen years.

I would like to thank all the women who have taken part in this book for agreeing to pose and be photographed and share their wartime experience over a cup of tea and cake, and for welcoming my project with open hearts.

Thanks to my MA photography teacher, Eti Wade, who always pushed me to go further and my fellow students who encouraged the idea. My thanks to John, Luc, Pierre and James for their support in letting me travel the country and devote time to this project. Also to my parents, who extended my knowledge and curiosity, living in an open-minded house where history and politics were always topics for debate. To my grandmother, Marie Louise, for letting me rummage through her photo box and telling me about her teenage years living under Nazi rule.

To my aunt Lydie for her support, to Jen Davies and Steve O'Neill who helped me kick start this whole project, to Catherine Mandiaux, Amar Grover and Pascale Szwagrzak for their enthusiastic support and precious help with editing. To all the people who have crossed my path for this project and have helped keep things moving forward. To all the men and women who have given their lives for freedom and democracy and made Europe a better place to live.

NB: While the women's stories have been lightly edited, when presenting them I have as far as possible left their recollections in their own words, so that you may hear their voices as clearly as I did when I was listening to them. Please remember that these are conversational, not literary, accounts.

FOREWORD

I have always felt a fascination with the Second World War; I was drawn to it, hooked by the diplomatic struggle happening before it even started. Learning about this historical period was like undoing the knots, one by one, of a very tangled detective story. If you have seen the film The Remains of the Day [1] it gives a good impression of the state of mind of those contemporaries who might have been tempted to endorse National Socialism in the context of the biggest economic crisis of all time. Indeed, it was not only the complicated

Rene Hornung (right), incorporated in the Malgre-Nous

international relationships that drove my curiosity, it was the secrecy and complexity behind the untold tales, like "Fortitude",[2] a whole operation dedicated to making

the Germans believe that the Allies were preparing a landing in the Pas-de-Calais. Fortitude was one of a larger network of dummy operations under the "Bodyguard" [3] umbrella. Even the agents on this mission did not know it was all a deception; effectively they were "sacrificed" to hide Operation Overlord (the D-Day landings).

Alsace, the region where I come from in France, paid a high price during this period and was annexed as German territory. When I was ten my grandfather taught me some Russian words he had learnt in Russia during the war. It did not really dawn on me why my grandfather was in Russia at the time, it sounded too complicated to understand. It was only when I started to browse through my grandmother's photo box that some disturbing images started to emerge of my grandfather in German army uniform with a swastika on his arm. How was it that my French grandfather was involved with the Germans? A shock, to say the least; it contrasted greatly with what I had learnt at school. We were taught that everybody in France was heroic and fought in the Resistance.

At the time I had never heard of the Vélodrome d'Hiver [4]; I would later discover that France's involvement in the Second World War was not so black and white after all. It was only in 1995 that the then French President Jacques Chirac officially acknowledged the Vichy French government's public responsibility for the deportation of 13,000 French Jews. Not a single German was involved in this operation. An excellent novel by Tatiana de Rosnay, Sarah's Key,[5] is a shocking illustration of the atrocities of the 'Vel d'Hiv'.

[1]   Film by James Ivory (1993)
[2]   Fortitude was the code name of a military deception during WWII, and part of an overall deception strategy called Bodyguard
[3]   Code name of a high level WWII deception plan
[4]   Velodrome d'Hiver (Vel d'Hiv)
[5]   Tatiana de Rosnay, Tatiana, Elle s'appelait Sarah, Héloise d'Ormesson, Paris, December 2008

In the final year of my baccalaureate I had a history teacher called Mrs Fabre who used to entertain us during class by relating her own experience of the war as a child in German-occupied Strasbourg. She recounted this with amusing sarcasm to help us understand that there were two types of citizen at the time: those who were allowed to speak French and those who were not. Obviously those collaborating with the Germans had the privilege of being allowed to continue speaking French in "this part of Germany" while everybody else had to conform to the Germanic way, even to the extent of having to change their first name to something less Gallic. Listening to Mrs Fabre was fascinating. I loved the way she made modern history so relevant by adding her own personal experience in the picture, and history quickly became my favourite subject.

The first time I heard about the "Malgré-Nous" [6] was probably around that time. I had read in the local newspapers about a German prisoner of war camp in Russia called Tambov. Here a number of Alsatians who had been forcibly enrolled in the German army never made it back, despite the efforts of General de Gaulle to try to make the Russians understand that these were French citizens who did not voluntarily fight in the German uniform and were under threat of having their entire family deported if they refused. I guess Stalin had other preoccupations at the time. Alsatians were certainly not the only population enrolled under duress. The last ones were eventually freed in 1956. As a result of this forced enrolment, applied from 25th August 1942 [7] my grandfather René was one of 100,000 Alsatians made to fight Josef Stalin's army; he spent two years in Russia fighting with the Wehrmacht.

For many years we were taught at school that France fought alongside the Allies against the Axe, General de Gaulle was our hero and that every French person joined the Resistance. This raised many questions about how my family fitted into this seemingly perfect French

Suzo Terribile

version of the war. My grandmother, Marie-Louise, remembers how scared she was of men in black uniforms (worn by the Waffen-SS): "They could send you to the Struthof-Natzweiler [8] and had right of life and death over anyone, and it was scary." A few years later I discovered that a very close member of my family, Suzo Terribile (also called Pascal), joined the Foreign Legion at twenty to fight with the Free French Army. Unfortunately I never had the chance to meet Suzo; he died in a fight when he was stationed in Marseille before going back to his base in Algeria in May 1945. I only recently tracked down his story; through some incredible luck and determination, I finally found him, having being close to despair that I would ever trace him.

The idea I had of the Second World War as a child was very different from the reality; nothing was as it seemed. French people chose to collaborate with the enemy, the French police were involved in deportation,

[6]   "In spite of our will"
[7]   From 25th August 1942, 100,000 Alsatians and Mosellans were drafted into the German armed forces
[8]   A German concentration camp located in the Vosges Mountains close to the Alsatian village of Natzwiller in France and the town of Schirmeck, about 50 km south from the city of Strasbourg

Alsatians were enrolled by force into the German army, allied agents had lost their lives for the sake of secrecy, and I am sure there is more to be untangled. The war brought us heroic images of men fighting at the front, young men sacrificing their lives to free Europe; it was very emotional to see my father shedding a tear when watching the movie The Longest Day [9].

Often missing from our heroic view of the war, however, is the role played by women. Without them countries would have come to a standstill; there would have been no trains, no buses, no munitions factories; the list goes on. Perhaps they are better recognised in the UK, but I came to wonder how women fitted into this otherwise heroically masculine war. It was only when I moved from France to England in 1998 that I learned more about the role that women played in supporting the war effort in World War II. I knew about women joining the Resistance, but had never really questioned my history lessons, had never wondered who helped the country move forward while the men were at war.

At the time I had just had my first child and being stuck at home with a small baby, I felt quite isolated. I decided to improve my English by studying for a BA in English. Four years and two more boys later, I chose to write my research essay, "Women's Contribution to the Second World War Effort". In a nutshell, it started with volunteers but after conscription at the end of 1941 the vast majority of the UK's women were enrolled in the services, factories and farming. Some took part in fully-fledged operations as agents with the Special Operations Executive (SOE), some ferrying Spitfires from one end of the country to the other. Having gone back to full-time work after rearing a young family, I somehow let the subject lie dormant until seven years later, when I decided to study for an MA in photography. It became clear that my photography project would be on women who had volunteered in the services, although little did I imagine the challenges I would be confronted with.

I started my research at the end of 2010, trying to trace women involved in the voluntary services via different associations, putting ads in magazines, and getting in touch with the Imperial War Museum. I knocked on many doors. I was sometimes lucky, sometimes not, but somehow persistence paid off.

Having graduated, I continued getting in touch with volunteers; two years on, having trawled the country from south to north and east to west, I have met the most amazing people, all willing to help me with this project. I have met amazing women, all in their late eighties and early nineties, still getting out and about, though some of them having difficulties with movement. Others remain young at heart. I remember being welcomed by Elizabeth Clifton in her Ferrari-red Fiat 500 at Morpeth station. I wanted to create this book to share the fascinating stories. I do hope that they will inspire you as they have me. For many of the women, these were the best years of their lives; however you look at it, this was an important part of their – and our – history.

[9]   A film directed by Ken Annakin, Andrew Marton, Bernard Wicki, Gerd Oswald, Darryl F. Zanuck

A WORD ABOUT THE SERVICES

Women started to be organised with the Women's Voluntary Service (WVS) as early as 1938, with about 290,000 enlisting as volunteers. The generation that had experienced the First World War knew how dreadful the war was, but often their daughters would see this period as an opportunity for change. The war held different implications for them, depending on their age, social and marital status. Once the war broke out the general reaction was fear, mostly concerning the changes the war would bring, but many young and single women looked on it as a chance to escape, the opportunity to leave the family home, to volunteer in an Army Corps or look forward to any alternative other than marriage. The arrogance of their youth made them look on war as a

prospect rather than a major fear. It does not sound obvious, but the Government experienced difficulties in recruiting volunteers. One of the problems that made it difficult was that the advertisements were written with a masculine perspective. "Serve with the Men who Fly", explaining that women were needed to fill the gap left by men, was not a very positive way to encourage them to work. Of the 300,000 volunteers who had registered by 1941, only 56,000 were women had volunteered to join the armed forces.

Motivations of those who volunteered

Many explained that this was an opportunity to move away from home while doing their bit for the country. Many volunteered against their parents' will, even forging their signatures. When I met Peggy Drummond-Hay [1], who volunteered in the Women's Voluntary Auxiliary Air Force (WAAF), she explained that she had volunteered via an ad in the Daily Express without telling her mother. "I did not tell her because she would not have agreed," she explained. "When I told her she nearly had a fit and told me that I was far too young to apply. I was seventeen at the time."

Pip Brimson chose to volunteer because she was inspired by the Battle of Britain and had a huge admiration for the Royal Air Force (RAF). In April 1941 the Government took a step towards conscription; all women born in the 1920s were required to register for employment if they were not already in paid, full-time service with the armed forces, or in the nursing or auxiliary services. The purpose of registration was to find new recruits, possibly free to move around the country, mainly for nursing and auxiliary services, the Navy, Army and Air Forces Institutes (NAAFI) and the

[1]   I met Peggy during my research for the BA in 2002

Women's Land Army [2]. Once registered, they were asked to come to a selection interview. The general view was that women should not throw up their present jobs unless they felt they were not serving the country in their present employment [3]. Three hundred thousand registered on April 19th, 1941.

The Conscription Act of December 1941

This affected all unmarried women between twenty and thirty and required them to register for work with the Labour Exchange Office. They could apply for work in either the services or factories. Most of them were required to be mobile and were employed according to labour shortages. Five million positions in civil employments were left vacant by men after they left for the war.

How did women contribute in the services?

Women could apply for work in the services, although some were difficult to get into, mainly because they did not lack volunteers. The Women's Royal Naval Service, for example, would only allow in girls who had family links with the navy. The services also had a problem with image.
The ATS was considered to be low key, somewhere you would replicate the work of a housewife, mostly caring and cleaning. With a better insight into the ATS, however, while this might have been true at first, ATS volunteers could also land jobs in the Special Executive Office, which required high-powered, skilled women to work as undercover agents or ferry aeroplanes for the ATA. Among a staff of 13,200

at the SOE, 3,200 were women. In total 418 were recruited as agents, 90 were trained to be sent over to France, and 39 were actually sent there. The first woman ever to be sent there was Yvonne Rudellat, whose code name was Jacqueline.

Women joining the forces were mostly middle class, educated and young. For them, entering the army was rather appealing because of the prestige attached to the names 'air force' and 'navy'. The number of women employed in the armed forces and auxiliary services increased from 56,000 in June 1940 to 466,400 in June 1944, a staggering rise of 800%. The majority of volunteers were aged between eighteen and twenty-one. At first it was assumed that women would stay in low key positions; "the first WRNS were only allowed into five categories involving various forms of clerical or domestic work and the situation was much the same in the WAAF"[4]. Until June 1942, WAAF volunteers were recruited only as clerks and cooks. If women were first pushed into menial work requiring no training, it was quite difficult to keep them there due to the increasing demand for workers to replace men; by not allowing them to occupy positions in more skilled areas, the country was suffering. As a result the government opened a training school for women.

The ATS

Established as the women's branch of the army, the Auxiliary Territorial Services (ATS) was set up in 1938 based on the remains of the Women's Auxiliary Army Corp (WAAC), set up during WWI. Between the two wars its name changed to Women's Transport Service (WTS) and it was later incorporated in the ATS. In 1939, when the menace of war was close, women volunteering to join the ATS were trained for duties in anti-aircraft batteries. The age limit to join was between seventeen and forty-three, but veterans of the First World War were accepted up to the age of fifty. At the outbreak of war the ATS went to the field with the Territorial Army; their

[2]   Labour Correspondent, Vital Working Waiting for Women: Registration on Saturday, The Times, 14th April 1941; 1-6

[3]   Labour Correspondent, Vital Working Waiting for Women: Registration on Saturday, The Times, 14th April 1941; 34-36

[4]   Waller, Jane and Vaughan Rees, Michael, 'Women in Uniform 1939-1945', Papermac, 1989, p. 56

main objective was to serve the army with household work, mostly cooking, storekeeping and paperwork.

In 1941 the ATS became part of the armed forces, with 65,000 members; by May 1945 they had reached 190,000, among them some very famous names, including Princess Elizabeth and Mary Churchill, Winston Churchill's youngest daughter. From 1942, the First Aid Nursing Yeomanry (FANY, which was now a branch of the ATS) started to serve the Special Operations Executive (SOE), where they took different positions as secretaries and also wireless operators. In 1949 it became the Women's Royal Army Corps and was integrated in all corps in 1990.

The Women's Auxiliary Air Force (WAAF)

The group formed in late June 1939 after splitting from the ATS, and Jane Trefusis was appointed as Air Commandant. Before 1941 women aged between eighteen and forty-three could enlist. After 1941 the age limit was extended to between seventeen and a half and forty-four and a half.

The women were posted in units all over Britain. 8,800 joined the WAAF at the first call for volunteers and, by 1943, they substituted men in some eighteen officers' categories and sixty-three airmen trades.

They served as radar operators, plotting reports in the control room, transferring information to visual plaques on racks, then positioning onto maps. They looked after parachute packing, manned barrage balloons and saw to catering, meteorology, telephones and telegraphs. Their most important role was maintenance and observation; German-speaking WAAFs were trained to imitate Luftwaffe fighter controllers, their main task being to give contradictory instructions to German night-fighters. As the RAF could not come to terms with the idea of women commanding combat planes, they were not allowed to fly fighter planes. However, they were accepted as pilots for the Auxiliary Transport Aviation (ATA).

The WAAF did not see a shortage of volunteers; in 1943 there were more than 180,000, and a quarter of a

Jane Eldridge served in the WRNS

million women had served in the WAAF. Their number constantly increased until 1944. After the war their number dropped drastically and only 517 remained in uniform by January 1950. In 1959 they changed their name to Women of the Royal Air Force and were finally allowed to gain their flying brevet. In 1994 they were completely integrated into the RAF.

The Auxiliary Transport Aviation

The ATA was set up by Commander Gerard d'Erlanger for pilots who lacked the qualifications to go into the RAF. In 1940, nine women were accepted as ATA pilots.

They ferried small open-cockpit aeroplanes at the beginning of the war and from 1941 they were allowed to ferry four-engine bombers. In total, women made up 25% of all the ATA pilots, and there were 156 women pilots in the ATA.

The Women's Royal Navy Service (WRNS)

The service was linked to the Royal Navy and set up in 1939 by permission of King George VI on a voluntary basis to replace naval officers' duties. The WRNS was the most prestigious of all the services in which women could volunteer, but also the most difficult to get into. To join they had to prove family connections with the navy and agree to be on a two-week probation period before enrolling.

This made the WRNS quite exclusive and the first choice for volunteers. For Gwendoline Page, author of Growing Pains: "Many girls had chosen to join the WRNS because of the three women's services the WRNS uniform was the most attractive, [...] more flattering to most girls' figures than more bulky uniforms of the ATS and the WAAF"[1].

Women were posted to naval ports like Chatham, Portsmouth, Devonport and Rosyth. Their role was to handle communications, write reports, be motor transport drivers, cooks, stewards, cipher officers and officers in charge. In 1941 they were allowed to serve abroad and their first mission was Gibraltar and Washington DC with the British Admiralty Delegation. In 1942 they were first sent to the Middle East and Alexandria, then later to the Far East, and they joined the Conference of Allied Nations in Yalta.

Although women were keen to participate in combat, to serve on fighter planes or battleships, they were not yet allowed to do so. Even though some women trained as sea rangers on HMS Implacable, they served on hospital ships only as nurses.

The WRNS was the smallest service to take on women. At the beginning of the war only 5,000 volunteers joined, reaching a total of 884,300 by the end

Ginge Thomas served in the WRNS

of the war. The fact that they were mostly posted in ports did limit the number of those able to join. If women were not allowed on combat vessels, it is important to note the role of women in the Merchant Navy, which was not opposed to having women working on board. Many women were serving on the "Front Line" in the Merchant Navy as stewardesses, nurses, shop assistants, pursers, doctors and engineers. These women were not volunteers, but had previously served on a navy ship; this kind of story serves as evidence against the argument of women serving on combat planes and battleships.

The Navy, Army and Air Force Institutes (NAAFI)

With its motto "Servant of those who serve", the purpose of the NAAFI was to serve the troops and by April 1940, 1,400 canteens had been set up. They took their origins from the old expeditionary canteens, and because the institutes were run conjointly with the three services, staffs were considered as civilians attached to the services. Their duties included serving, but also cooking for the troops and selling chocolate, toiletries

[1] Gwendoline Page, Growing Pains: A teenager's war, The Book Guild Lewis, 1994, 86

and polish. They also provided an important element to the troops – entertainment and dances until around 12 midnight. As the war progressed the girls were often asked to undertake other types of work outside their usual duties at the canteen, like unpacking cooking equipment and bedding in horrible winter weather. Towards the end of the war some of the girls were sent abroad with troops.

The nursing services

The work and dedication of nurses during the First World War gave immediate recognition to women who chose to volunteer with the Voluntary Aid Detachment (VAD). The VADs were formed in 1908 with young women joining the British Red Cross Society or St John Ambulance Brigade. They formed the civil nursing reserve with trained army nurses. They were usually sent to military hospitals with a very basic training of only ninety hours and a few lectures, so desperate was the need for nurses. Each army had their own trained army nurses. The army recruited QAIMNS (Queen Alexandra's Imperial Military Nursing Service); the navy, QARNNS (Queen Alexandra's Royal Nursing Service) and the air force, PMRAFNS (Princess Mary's Royal Air Force Nursing Service). In total 324,900 women joined the nursing services in the army. The number of recruits saw a sharp rise in the years 1944-45.

Request for secret work
ULTRA

ULTRA was the code name used to designate the work done to decipher German messages coded with the Enigma machine. The first WRNS to be appointed for work at Bletchley Park, also called Station X, arrived in March 1941. The cipher officers working for the WRNS were coded under the designation "Ultra". The function of the two thousand women working under Ultra was considered to be higher than top secret; Ruth Bourne (p. 52) was not allowed to speak about her assignment at

Bletchley Park until 1972. Station X was a combined operation between the army, navy, RAF and civilians, who all worked in separate departments (women from the ATS and the WAAF were appointed to operate Typex machines). The main role of the Ultra team members was to decode messages from the German Enigma machine and run huge computing machines called "bombes", the most powerful of the time (the WRNS were first chosen to operate the bombes as an experiment). These messages originated from the German army, navy, air force and Command Headquarters. One of the requirements of those positions was that all volunteers should keep their work secret.

The Special Operation Executive (SOE)

After the Dunkirk evacuation the MP Hugh Dalton sent a memorandum to the Foreign Secretary to stress the need for a special operations service: "We have to organise movements in enemy-occupied territory comparable to the Sinn Fein movement in Ireland [...]. The aim should be to coordinate, inspire, control and assist nationals in oppressed countries, we need absolute secrecy, a certain fanatical enthusiasm, willingness to work with people of different nationalities, complete political reliability" [2]. This encouraged the War Cabinet to approve formation of the Special Operation Executive in July 1940. The same year, Colonel Gubbins – who become chief of the SOE in 1943 and General of the Inter-Services Research Bureau – made contact with Phyllis Bingham, the commander of the First Aid Nursing Yeomanry (FANY) service. The colonel "wanted to know if she could provide some personnel for highly secret work" [3]. For a start, the new recruits were to serve as escort officers to agents in training, working on producing passports, ration cards and forged documents, packing arms and sabotage equipment, typing and filing.

By the end of the war, half the women played important parts in the work of SOE. If most of them occupied clerical and administrative positions, some of

[2] Beryl E. Escott, Mission Improbable: A Salute to the RAF Women of the SOE in Wartime France, Sparkford: Patrcik Stefens Limited, 1991, 45.
[3] Beryl E. Escott, Mission Improbable: 64

Nancy Cooper - Volunteer in the Land Army

agents of section F (France), were praised for their contribution to the war effort and decorated with the Croix de Guerre and Member of the Order of the British Empire (MBE). Four women agents died in the camp of Struthof-Natzweiler in Alsace.

Women's Land Army

The WLA was a civilian organisation created by the Board of Agriculture in 1915 to replace the men who were called up to war. It started again in 1939. Women in the Land Army were completing a different job from those in the armed forces. Land Army volunteers and workers were recruited to carry on with farm work. This included care of animals, spreading muck and rat catching, jobs that men had usually done before the war. Between June 1939 and 1945 the number of women employed in agriculture increased by 83%. In June 1940, 8,800 had volunteered for the Land Army and by 1944 the number of women in the Land Army had risen to 78,000; the last WLA were disbanded in 1950. The Women's Timber Corp worked in the forestry industry and were known as the "Lumber Jills".

them were brave enough to pioneer as undercover agents. Yvonne Rudellat and Noor Inyat Kahn, two

WOMEN WHO SERVED

JOY LOFTHOUSE

Pilot, ATA, 1941 to 1945

"My only interest in flying was through my boyfriends; all were pilots in training. No one flew before the war unless they were very wealthy. Where we are in this part of the country, we are surrounded by airfields; Little Rissington, Aston Down and Kemble. I was reading *The Aeroplane*, it is a monthly magazine, still going, and it said that the ATA had run out of qualified pilots and they were training *ab initio*. I applied and got in; at the time I didn't even drive a car!"

Did you have to pass an exam?
"No, but you had to be five foot six inches tall, and pass a medical, of course. In the interview they were looking to see if you would be a good supporting member of the team. They were asking for coordination and wanted certain academic qualifications to know that you were reasonably educated. The early people got in just on their flying – if you could fly, you were in. My sister also got in, we were the only two sisters flying. There was no influence, she applied from a different address with a different name; she was already a war widow, her husband had been killed after a year's marriage.

"They trained me at a small airfield in Oxfordshire. I spent most of my flying time at Hamble, near Southampton, because it was close to the factory at Eastleigh that turned out the Spitfires. These airfields were called "pools" because they were near the factory. Our job was to fly the aeroplanes coming out of the factory. Any plane might have to be moved from anywhere to anywhere. Towards the end of the war I got on to light twin-engines, including the *Oxfords*.

"The war ended too soon; I was not one of the girls who flew big heavies, although I flew twenty-eight different types of aircraft altogether. They gave us a licence such as pre-war flyers had, but very few women were able to do anything after the war because the men wanted their jobs back. Women just had a role in the war; after the war they were expected to go back to what they'd done before. People hardly believe it nowadays, but pre-war in this country you had to leave teaching when you were married.

"In the 1950s Dan Air [1] took women for the first

[1] Dan Air Services was an airline that operated in the UK from 1953

time; in the forties there was very little opportunity. We like the idea that we were the trailblazers."

How long was the training?
"First you flew a Magister [2], then you spent some time in a Harvard [3], then you went on to the Spitfire. After that you were fully trained, you'd gone from being a cadet to a fully-fledged officer. In 1945 I went on conversion to twin engine aircraft."

The best you remember?
"I suppose the first flight in the Spitfire; we were only three years away from the Battle of Britain and of course you knew that once you had flown, you would not be thrown out. Everybody loved the Spitfire, it was the little lady of the single engine; it was so easy to manoeuvre, such a compact cockpit. You were alone in the cockpit when you flew everything. When you trained you had an instructor behind you. Once you'd gone solo, you had an instructor again to teach you to do forced landings; they would shut the throttle and make you come out of a spin. Once you were working you were alone, even when you were picking up a Barracuda [4], which in service would have an observer on board; when we flew them, we were alone."

How did your parents react?
"They were very proud of us, of course, but I think at first they were worried. I had two sisters and I think my dad was pleased he had no sons to go to war. He still ended up with two of his daughters in the services, but I am sure when he saw us in uniform, he was very proud."

Did you know how many flights you had to do?
"Well, it just depended on the weather. We didn't work nine to five, we worked for a couple of weeks then we had three days off, not necessarily on weekends. They were always very good; if they knew you were going on leave, they would give you some kind of flight near your home and I was lucky because there were so many airfields around. I was at Hamble all the time until spring

1945, when there was less and less work and some of the pools were closing. Some of the men were only too happy to leave – solicitors, managers, people running their own business, etc – but I never wanted to leave; I was happy.

"So I was sent up to Yorkshire, to Sherburn-in-Elmet, near Leeds. I did a lot of Fleet Air Arm work, flying planes up to Scotland to go on the aircraft carriers. As far as I was concerned, no one knew about the bomb, unlike today. After VE day, the aircraft carriers had to go to the Far East; they were still fighting their way across the Pacific Islands and we all thought we had to invade Japan, the way we had invaded Europe. Then the bomb came. Of course, it was dreadful, but we would have still lost millions of people if we'd had to invade Japan, because of the way they kept fighting, so I was doing that work until VJ day and I came out in September of 1945. It was the last time I flew; the ATA was a wartime thing, it did not exist afterwards. We weren't even forces; we did not swear allegiance to the King's Commission, we were civilians in uniforms. We were paid by the Ministry of Aircraft Production. It was started by a director of the British Overseas Airline Corporation (BOAC), the forerunner of British Airways.

"The men came in 1939; it was not until 1940 that they let women in and then they gave them a special place near the Tiger Moth factory at Hatfield. They flew as trainers, and did that for almost a year, and it was not until 1941 that the first lady flew a Hurricane. I suppose they proved themselves on the training plane and I've read that we were the first women to get equal pay for equal work, although I don't think it lasted after the war. We had a very good commandant for the ladies section, called Pauline Gower; she was a pre-war flyer who had done 2,000 hours, and she was in the right position to stand up for the women in the ATA."

Did you continue to fly after the war?
"No, no, I just got married and had a family. I suppose after six years of war – it was a wartime job – in those days one was rather off the shelf if you weren't married

[2] Magister aircraft   [3] Harvard aircraft   [4] Barracuda aircraft

by your thirties, we did not have the opportunity of having a career. We were quite content with our lot; there were 156 women pilots in the ATA, we had a couple of navigators, all air crew, all pilots, and there were about 900 men. We did the same job as the men; of course, they did a bit more because they had a lot more pre-war experience. A lot of them got on the four-engine planes. I think we had about eight women who did the same, they were the ones who were in early on. There are still a few of us left. There is an ATA association, although we did not come together for twenty-seven years, when we had a reunion dinner at RAF Lyneham. We are still in touch, but there aren't too many of us left; we have half-a-dozen in nursing homes. Those who joined when the war broke out are all in their nineties. I was sixteen-and-a-half when the war broke out and it is because I am still walking and talking that I get called up to do so many things."

Any special anecdotes?

"The most notable ones were on D-Day. For weeks before, the south coast was closed because of the build-up for D-Day; you could have walked across to the Isle of Wight on the landing barges. I assumed the Germans could see them from high range reconnaissance, but they thought we would come in from the Pas-de-Calais. On the morning of the sixth of June, one that flew saw that the whole of the Solent was empty, all the boats were gone."

What about all those people on the beaches?

"One did not realise the dreadful time they had to go through, but at least one felt it had to be done, it was the next stage in the war. We weren't going to win it until we went back into Europe. The weather was our worst enemy; because we had no radio, you were flying blind if you lost your horizon.

"I had one or two shaky moments. They had put in a Griffin engine with 2,400 horsepower and one of the girls told me on my first Griffin flight, "open up very gently or she will sweep full rudder". I did it all and I was still making it for the Southampton barrage balloons! It was only for a second, it felt like a minute, until she got up into the air.

"People were amazed that we could go from one aeroplane to another, but it's only the same as going from one car to another; we were young, nothing fazed us. These were our formative years, it was the time we were supposed to be at university; it was an amazing experience, you can say that. It was amazing, amazing, you can't describe the experience of flying, or dealing with some of the difficulties. Some test pilots said about the Spitfire it was a lady in the air but a bitch on the ground, because she had a very high nose, yet she had quite a low undercarriage. If we had to land into the wind it was hard to do. My sister broke one Spitfire, she tried to land with a crosswind, a tyre blew off and she touched with the undercarriage, but she said, "All I broke is a fingernail!"

"We were probably a little nervous the first time we flew but, as I said, we had the confidence of youth. I sometimes feel in recent years, why do we get so much fuss made about us, because every woman worked at something and there were some women who worked for six years, Sundays included, in factories and got no rewards at all? Nobody said they did a good job, we were just the lucky ones as we got the praise for it, but I don't think we necessarily deserved it. We had the bravery of youth, that's about all, but I am sure anybody else could have done the same thing."

PHYLLIS "GINGER" THOMAS

WRNS, 1943 to 1946; part of Operation Overlord

Phyllis Thomas lives in Wales in a small retirement flat. I was welcomed by her niece, Becca, who got in touch with me to schedule the meeting. When I met Phyllis, she was resting in her armchair and she had already prepared a lot of documents and press cuttings from her time in the army. It was only when she showed me headings about General Morgan that I understood that Phyllis had been working close to the top; she was an assistant for General Morgan [1] the genius behind Operation Overlord [2]. Phyllis, or 'Ginge', as she is known, worked in a town clerk's office in Swansea. In March 1943, at the age of twenty-two, she joined the WRNS.

"You could not be called up to the WRNS, they had a different system to the other services with a fortnight's probation. If you liked it you could stay, if you didn't you could join another service. I really wanted to join because my boss was due to retire and I fancied the navy blue uniform."

Ginge showed me a few of her press cuttings; she was featured on thisissouthwales.co.uk [3] and received a letter from King George V (see p.7) praising her work in the navy. She confided in me, "I am terribly sorry to say, but I enjoyed my war." I explained that it makes sense, all the women I spoke to said they'd had a fantastic time, despite the hardship and the dreadful price the men paid at the front.

How did your parents react when you joined?
"My mother died when I was born; my family did not mind. It was only the second time I'd been to London, I was twenty-two." (Becca told me her aunt was amazed that I'd come all the way from London to speak to her.)

How did you end up working for Morgan?
"The WRNS headquarters was somewhere between Belsize Park and Chalk Farm. I was part of a typing pool at Norfolk House and was originally assigned to the naval section. After just a few days I was on loan to different sections. I went to meet General Morgan, the Chief of Staff to the Supreme Allied Commander, or COSSAC. He said, "Hello, sailor," sat down and gave me

[1] Frederick E. Morgan (1894-1967) Chief of Staff to the Supreme Allied Commander (COSSAC), the original planner of Operation Overlord
[2] Code name for the Battle of Normandy.
[3] 30 May 2004

a letter to type. My first impressions of the general were that he was quite tall, with fair hair and almost boyish looks, and with a lovely soft voice, very easy to take dictation from. He was very friendly. One day I spoke to Churchill on the phone, he said, 'Morgan' and mumbled. General Morgan was working in the office in the room next to me and I can tell you, he was gorgeous (you can see a common theme here). That was the beginning of what turned out to be not only a wonderful job, but a wonderful friendship as well. He called me "sailor" until the day he died. The Supreme Allied Commander hadn't yet been appointed and I soon realised that it was General Morgan who was responsible for planning the assault on the Continent.

"My work depended on whatever was going on. I usually had to attend the Chief of Staff's conferences in the morning and evening and the rest of the time I dealt with anything the General wanted answered or typed. After the morning meetings everything had to be typed up for the evening, and after the evening meetings everything had to be typed for the following morning, so there was very little time off. We often worked into the early hours of the morning. The atmosphere in Norfolk House was very focused, everyone seemed to be concentrating on the job, so there were no little cliques standing around and talking. There was always a feeling of confidence among the staff, there had to be, with an operation of that magnitude. Everything depended on getting it right, we knew that the lives of thousands of troops were at stake. Everyone worked very long hours, often well into the evening; you just worked when you had to work and left when you were told to go.

"I worked with General Morgan until the end of March 1944. In April of that year I was moved to Southwark House with the naval unit. We were given very short notice that we were moving and frantically packed all our bits and pieces. When I found out that General Eisenhower would be Supreme Allied Commander and that General Morgan would not be leading the invasion, I felt sad, but the General seemed happy about the choice of leader. I think he realised all

along that he was the Chief of Staff to the Supreme Commander Designate, that was the brief that had been given to him. He knew very well that someone else would be appointed and probably suspected that it would be an American.

"I moved on to work with Admiral Ramsay before the [D-Day] invasion. I was exactly a year with General Morgan, and from a work point of view we were on a rolling service. They sent me over by boat to France with Admiral Ramsay's office; near the coast of France we had to disembark onto landing craft and we landed in the wonderful Mulberry harbour. *(This was a portable temporary harbour developed by the British in World War Two to facilitate rapid offloading of cargo onto the beaches during the Allied Invasion of Normandy.)* [4] We had typed about it hundreds of times, but were now seeing it for the first time. I remember travelling through St Lô (Normandy) and being astonished at the amount of damage there had been to the place. I was used to bomb damage because Swansea had been badly damaged, but the devastation here was breathtaking.

As we travelled through Normandy, troops would stand outside their tents waving at us; they probably didn't see many girls around there! We were taken to billets somewhere in Normandy and after a few days we moved to Caen. While staying there I got in touch with General Morgan and his aide, Roland Harris, and I spent Christmas day with them. We had a wonderful time in France. We were under the umbrella of SHAEF (Supreme Headquarters Allied Expeditionary Force) and we were treated like lords and ladies; wonderful food, wonderful entertainment in the camps. We were invited by the French to lots of functions and sometimes dinner would take about three hours because the food would come in about seven different courses. In the place we stayed we had a bathroom with gold taps. We were free to go into Paris. I remember going into Paris on the Metro quite often, we would visit The Galeries Lafayette and other wonderful places. I loved the Sacré-Coeur and visited it very often. Later we went to Germany, to Linden (Hesse, Germany); we were not asked if we

[4] Source Wikipedia

wanted to come over, we were just told to do so. *(Ginge excuses herself for forgetting some details, reminding me, "I am ninety-two, you know.")* The Germans welcomed us in their houses for us to be housed, I don't know what I was expecting but people were lovely to us."

Did you have access to secret information?

"Yes. We were even escorted going to the loo when we had to type about invasion plans. We were sworn to secrecy, there were code names for different areas, we were using shorthand, I used to go to sleep singing songs in shorthand. We could not use Dictaphones, shorthand was essential then. I don't know if they destroyed any documents… they might have, but we were not involved in that."

"During that time at Norfolk House, an appeal went out to the public to send in postcards of the coast of Normandy, or maps, Michelin Guides or any other information that might help with the planning of the operation. Although I didn't personally have anything to do with sorting out the information that was sent in, I remember the rooms with postcards stuck on the walls. When I first received my uniform they were all cut for the average person of five foot nine or ten; I was only five foot three! The waist went down to the top of my legs; I had to use safety pins to keep it at my waist. For the bras, they said, "What size are you?" I said, "Thirty-six inches." He replied, "We only have thirty-two inches or forty-two inches." The bloomers were close to the knees, it just gives you this lovely picture! When I was in France I came about to speak to General Montgomery. Two American soldiers guarded the gate and looked at me; when I asked to see him, one of them said, 'Oh, yes, and I am the King of England!' I said, 'Go out and find out, then,' to their dismissal."

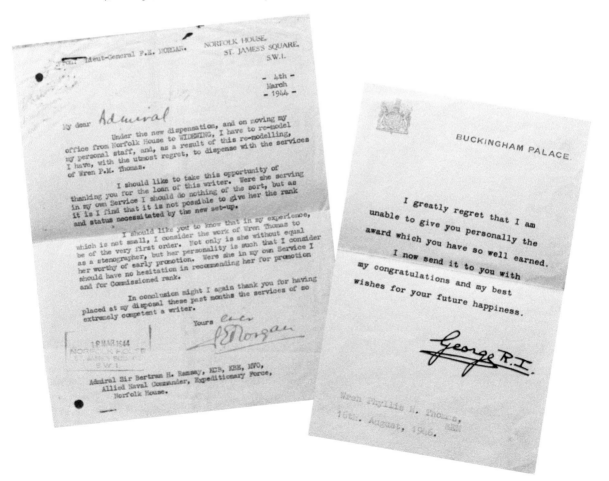

What was the best you remember about your experience?

"It was the comradeship, really … you know, there was no bickering, no nastiness, no bitchiness, it was unusual indeed. Everybody would help; I had a wonderful time. At first I thought, what am I going to do here? After the fortnight's training you were allocated to a certain area. I was sent for some tests, and the first thing I was asked to do was clean the toilets instead of doing the test! They had sent me to the wrong headquarters at the wrong address. When they called where I was supposed to be, I was missing, and I thought, I will spend my life cleaning the toilets! We had to do things, it was to keep you occupied for the two weeks training, they could ask you to scrub the dance floor down on your knees with French polish. To some extent it was probably a test to show that you were prepared to do anything.

"At the end of the war, General Morgan wanted me to join him in his new job, but by then I wanted to come home so I was demobbed in August 1946. My job in the town clerk's office was open for me, I got paid well when I was there and decided to go back to it. When I got out, I got a job with Swansea University; I worked twenty-five years there, I could not have been happier there. There was no incentive to stay in the WRNS, you didn't know what was going to happen."

Ginge acknowledges that people would not have the same sense of duty today.

" My husband was called up, he had to go, I don't think people would do that today. I received the British Empire Medal for my war service. I don't think General Morgan was ever given the credit he deserved. Winston Churchill made him famous in a simple sentence when he said that it was General Morgan of the British Army who had been primarily responsible for the invasion plans. It was our General Morgan who initiated it, but others subsequently got the credit for it. I kept in touch with the General after the war. We used to send letters and Christmas cards to each other. I still have a wonderful letter from him, which I cherish very much, in which he says, "Do you remember that it's eighteen years now since you and I put Ike on the road to victory?"

Any specific anecdotes?

"There is a story about my photograph (p.5). It was taken by a photographer for the WRNS, I never had a perm before I went into the WRNS. I had this perm - at the time you could have a perm for a bar of chocolate, a perm in those days took about five hours! I was asked to have my photograph taken because I had my hair done, but I didn't know what they wanted to use my photo for.

When I was in the training area for two weeks, in Mill Hill in London, I never managed to sort my right from my left during the army parades. When we were all called in to parade, she said, "Left turn, quick march," and I went on the complete opposite side; that was my first encounter. I did not go on another parade after that because of the job I had. We were more like civilians, we did not have to go on parade, it was more an office job."

GWEN JOWITT

Equipment clerk, WAAF, 1939-1942

I was introduced to Gwen by Diana Lindo (p. 41), who very kindly helped me to find more volunteers. I wrote to Gwen and another lady called Barbara; they both wrote back. Barbara wrote me a very long letter explaining that she was now too old to be photographed, but she talked about her time in the WRNS. Gwen, on the other hand, was up for it. I called her and explained what this project entailed. I would come to visit and interview her about her experience in the WAAF, and I also wanted to take her portrait. Many of the women found it quite odd having their portrait taken at such an advanced age and often would try to discourage me by saying, "But I am so old!"

Maybe we are at a loss at the idea of old people being photographed, but this project relied on photography and as a photographer it was essential for me to take a portrait of the person they are today, not only to have a copy of their image during their time in uniform. How they would speak about their experience in the WRNS, the WAAF or another service was also part of who they are today; they certainly would have expressed it differently at the time.

Two weeks before our meeting, Gwen suddenly got cold feet and explained that she had difficulty walking and it would be too difficult for her to drive around looking for a war memorial or any other landmark worth using as a background. On the grounds of Gwen's reluctance I did not push it further, but instead called

her to ask if she would still agree to meet me and simply have her portrait taken near her house. Persistence paid off and she happily obliged.

On the day, as arranged at 1.30 pm, I was standing in front of Gwen's flat. She opened the door promptly and greeted me with a great smile. She was wearing an electric blue cardigan which lit up the blue of her eyes, and her hair was neatly set in waves around her face. The make-up and pearls were on, which meant she was ready to have her portrait taken. She offered me some food, which I had to decline, and suggested a coffee with some ginger cake; hard to refuse.

Gwen was very anxious to please and wanted the best for me; she was concerned that I had travelled all that way for nothing and that her story would be of no interest to me. I reassured her that this project was about women doing their bit for the country, she chose to be a volunteer, no one forced her to do it, and this was to be acknowledged, whatever she thought of it.

"When I look back, I was too quick; on the Sunday I was seventeen and you had to be eighteen to join." (she changed her date of birth on her application form and when the officer said, "Are you sure you are eighteen?" she said she was).

"You see, with Diana [Lindo], we both agreed that we should not have rushed into it, we should have taken more time to think about what we wanted to do, but we just went to register and our mouths dropped. 'I am ready to do anything', we said when we each replied about the positions we would like. I spent my youth in Shipley, a town with a military base, close to the navy dockyard, so joining the army myself was something it felt natural to do. Later I lived on the Isle of Sheppey [off the Northern Coast of Kent in the Thames estuary] which was a billeted town, army and navy. My father and uncles were in the navy, and I was used to being surrounded by army. I thought, God, this is a wonderful opportunity to join the air force!

"When the war broke out, on Monday I took the first train up to London. I'd never been to London before, you very much lived in the family in those days. I found the Air Ministry, and when I arrived there was a queue a mile long, all women wanting to join the air force, so I joined the queue and spent much of the day in it and eventually I was interviewed by a woman. She asked me what I wanted to do. Of course I did not have a clue, I should have spent time researching. I'd never had a job, I'd just left school, so I told her I was ready to do anything, which was madness. 'Would you like to work in equipment, as an equipment clerk?' I was asked; 'Oh, yeah,' I replied. So after my interview with the air officer I'd landed a job as an equipment clerk – I would be responsible for distributing the uniforms.

"I went to Hendon to train when I was joined up, that was just to do square-bashing [1] for a month or so, and then I was sent to the sorting office in Northolt. Everything was completely disorganised and we did not have uniforms at the beginning of the war. Not many people had jobs, we were getting sorted out. I went to Bridlington in Yorkshire for about a month to do the course to prepare for the job. I did not do a course earlier because nothing was organised. We had a raincoat and a beret and that was our uniform for several months; they gradually brought in uniforms, we've got the skirts there, you see? (see photograph p.13). Then I was stationed at a radar station in Kent called Dunkirk and it was mostly radar operators who worked there, which I was quite envious of. I have to say, I would have loved doing the job of the girls who were plotters, but I knew nothing of it because of not having researched jobs beforehand.

"I was there for about a year and enjoyed it enormously. I was doing clerical work and sometimes peeling potatoes. It was a very small unit, and we had two very well-known fighter stations nearby, Biggin Hill and Lansdowne (Kent). We had a very good time there, we were invited to dances and to all the sorts of entertainment they put on. When off duty we used to walk in Canterbury and you would see lots of Spitfires flying over your head; we got used to it and every now and then a parachute would come down. It was just so active.

"One day I was outside with a couple of WAAFs and we were joking and this plane came around very low, in a circle. We could see the pilot. The bomb doors opened, then we were running for our lives into the shelter; they did hit the radar stations and killed soldiers. It was a German plane, we were not clever enough to recognise the markings, it took us a while to get used to it. All the hospital vehicles from Dunkirk came driving through on the road to London.

"Later, I was sent to Cardington (Bedfordshire), a barrage balloon station. The balloons were acting as a protection against the place being bombed, they went up to stop the planes and prevented fighter planes flying low, and it did stop the bombing to a certain extent. Gosh, I hated it there, I couldn't stand the place! I wanted to be where the action was! I hated it so much that I took the first opportunity to be moved.

[1] square-bashing drill performance repeatedly on a barrack square

"I had been there a couple of weeks and there were several of us, we were over-staffed, too many WAAFs and not enough jobs. The sergeant came one day, and said, "There is a posting in Driffield, if you would like it?" Well, who was first in line? Me, because Driffield [East Yorkshire] was bomber command, you see. I volunteered immediately and they accepted; they had Wellington bombers and I loved it there. Everybody was absolutely fantastic. My mission there was to report on crews taking off. I worked on night duty with another WAAF, there was always two of us during the night. One evening I chatted to an Australian guy who explained, "we are just going on ops now." Of the seven planes that went, only the one with the Australian guy on board came back.

"About midnight, there was the most enormous noise over our roof, we rushed outside to see what it was and this plane had crashed about a hundred yards from us (Gwen gets very emotional). For a few seconds it was somehow silent, then airmen came from every direction to help the men in the plane get out, there were seven in there, but they could not get anywhere near because of the heat. The tail of the plane broke off when they landed and went across the airfield, and the only survivor was the rear gunner; all the others died. They had been flying to Germany and the plane had been hit mid-air. That night seven planes flew out and this was the only plane that came back and it crashed. It was so close, it was unbelievable, and it ended up crashing at the end of the runway. Just speaking to you brings everything back, those poor chaps, they were so young. Being on a station like that, this was not unusual, it happened quite a lot.

"For some time we had to share the mess with the sergeants and every once in while we would see new faces, knowing that the previous ones had all been killed and these young men were facing the same fate. It was so sad, all these young men. It was rather hard to take. This is what I felt again when I went to the war memorial in Runnymede; I lived it all over again, all those names of the men who have been killed, it all reminded me of how I felt when I looked at these boys in the mess at the time.

"When I was in Driffield, I did the most stupid thing; I just went off and got married! I had met Roderick before the war, we started to go out together right from the start, I knew him for quite some time. By this time three years had gone by, we were still seeing each other and spent the New Year's Eve together. We arranged to get married. My mother had already organised everything and then I got cold feet and decided not to do it. He was keener than me – this was 1942, I was nineteen by this time – and he came to see me, he did not want to take no for an answer! 'He's a proper control freak,' my officer said, 'off you go, sort yourself out!'

"I walked out of the station and he was standing there. He told me he loved me, and I loved him, but deep down I just knew it was not the right thing to do. But I said all right and we went to the local church, and of course we were under age, you had to be twenty-one to get married, so we both lied about our ages. The vicar agreed to marry us and invited us to stay with him. I got some of the girls to come down and we got married that afternoon. We went to stay at the sergeant's house, and that was the beginning of all my problems. Rod was stationed in Hereford, he was an armourer at time, he was a sergeant there. I applied for compassionate posting and I got it. I went to Hereford, which was very nice, I liked it a lot, but of course I got pregnant after three months and had to leave the air force – this was September 1942. I spent three years in Germany with Roderick, we came back to England and then he was posted back in Germany again. He met a German woman and we got divorced. In 1952 I remarried, we were married forty-seven years! My grandson went to Sandhurst."

How did you parents react?
"My father was in the navy. My mother encouraged me because she wanted to join the service in the First World War, but her father did not let her. They took it very well; my father was quite proud and I was used to service life. My daughter was an army nurse. I love the service life, my husband was a major in the army."

What was the best thing about being a volunteer?
"The best thing really was gaining my independence. It was nice meeting people from different lives, we had a lot of fun, we laughed a lot and we cried, because boyfriends got killed. We were such a close knit group, somebody would always help you; I wish I had made a career out of it."

BARBARA CAMPBELL

Recruiter and later statistician
officer, WAAF, 1941-1945

I went to visit Barbara on a very cold winter's day and was welcomed in Southend by a bitterly cold easterly wind. When I reached the front door, she somehow did not expect me and thought I was someone doing door-to-door calls. Once I explained and we went inside her house, she was very welcoming and eager to speak about her time in the WAAF.

Barbara joined in October 1941, aged seventeen and a half, and her first station was Innsworth, outside Gloucester.

What made you decide to join the services?

"Where we lived in Northampton, our house overlooked fields three miles out to Sywell aerodrome (Northamptonshire); a year before the war broke out we could watch all the training planes. We felt part of it, the gap between us and the airport was the air they were training in. My brother's friend joined the WAAF. I didn't fancy the army. Northampton region was the headquarters of the Northampton regiment, it was full of soldiers and I didn't like the ATS uniform; it was not as smart as the WAAF uniform.

"My father died when I was seven and my mother was a midwife, so she was never at home. There was very little home life. We were very conscious of the fact that we were needed [in the forces]. I was seventeen and a half when I went in. I reported to Innsworth I was there for four days being signed in, then given a uniform, and we went to train in Morecambe [Lancashire] where we were initiated into the WAAF. I had joined as a motor transport driver, but missed my posting to my training depot as I have had a flu.

"I was there for six weeks. One day we were all called to go to a cinema. A university professor gave us a lecture on new jobs, and those interested could stay behind to take a test, which I did; it was the same test we later gave to the forces. We took the tests in the morning, we got the grades in the afternoon. There were about a hundred of us in files, afterwards thirty-six of us were chosen, although you did not realise at the time that you had been chosen. We went to the Institute of Industrial Psychology at Oxford, stationed at Magdalen College, and trained there a couple of months, with a very intensive nine-to-five course. We were initiated into the job of aptitude testing. When they had to select people to do the jobs of engineers, wireless operators, they chose people that had the aptitude to pass the tests at that time.

"When we finished at Oxford we were divided into six groups and posted into the receiving depots, which were Carsington (Derbyshire), Ainsworth (Greater Manchester), Penarth (Wales), and Wilmslow (Cheshire). There were six WAAF and WRAF receiving depots. The headquarters was based in West Drayton. I was stationed there, but we were out in depots. As there were no WAAF training centres in Ireland, they wanted someone to be sent there, and they chose recruits who would be sent across for testing at Wilmslow.

"I was sent over to Ireland to start the initial recruitment process. Belfast was the only testing centre in Northern Ireland. We didn't test them in the receiving depot; the recruiting office in Belfast was the only place this test was done in the WAAF. I went out with a WAAF officer, who went over to do the interviews. I did the job aptitude testing. There was no pass on the aptitude, except if you were a blank idiot. The aptitude was more a triage. Some of it was English, some of it was maths, one was practical, there were three tests. You did not have to pass everything, it was the aptitude that counted, and also how you would have done in one test against the other; your aptitude for the job was determined by measuring one test against the others. There were five diagrams and you had to make up the sixth. The practical

one showed you two images and said, "did you flip or turn to make one into the other?" The purpose of these tests was more to determine at which job you would be best, your posting would be based on these test results, i.e. D was an aptitude for verbal spelling. There was further maths testing for radio mechanics. The work I did was considered to be confidential."

How many would pass the training exam?

"If they did not pass, they did not pass. I had no idea how many women would pass. From West Drayton I went down to Compton Bassett (Wiltshire) to wireless operating training. At the end of each course they would put back the one who did not pass and give them a little refresher. Every two months we went down to remaster those who did not pass. You did not know what was going on in the training school, because it had nothing to do with you."

How would women become officers?

"To start with they were Oxford graduates; most of them were people from university. Barbara Bond was an interviewer, she was with me in the recruiting offices in Belfast. She was a clerk to the board, secretary to the Commanding Officer. We were in a men's recruiting office, the majority came from Southern Ireland. The main dorms were up away in a field, the site was a WAAF site, we travelled by bikes. There was a Navy, Army and Air Forces Institute (NAAFI), and the next two sites were men's sites. The dorm was down the road; we were issued a bicycle, we could not have got around without that. I went back to Northern Ireland to do statistics training, then travelled around the country for my job to Belfast, Londonderry, Glasgow, Cumberworth (Lincolnshire).

"I met my husband just after D-Day. Northern Ireland was completely shut off at the time because of the imminence of D-Day and the fear of German spies being posted at the German Embassy in Southern Ireland. I came back to the UK in June 1944 to get married, and went to do statistics in the RAF offices in West Drayton. There were no computers at the time, everything was calculated by hand with a log book.

"I remember my time in WAAF as a wonderful time. I was promoted to sergeant. I used to go out to London during the time of the bombing, but hardly noticed the trouble at the time. The V1 made a noise like motorbikes flying over, it was more dramatic with the V2, as you did not hear any noise before the attack, there was complete silence a few seconds before they landed.

"I had my first baby in 1945 and came home to Northampton to join my husband, who was stationed in Cornwall. He belonged to the Royal Artillery Corps, in the coastal defence. With the war coming to an end, he was trained to be in a special contingent and they were positioned to relieve the Channel Islands. I knew once the war was finished that he would be posted over to the Channel Islands and he was there for three months. They did not really know when the Germans would give up; they got there a day before they discovered the war was finished. They were laid off until the Germans gave in and got their notice from Berlin.

"The Channel Islands were used as a recreation resort, the Germans used the place as a holiday resting place for the troops; this was Jersey and Guernsey, my husband went to Guernsey. He was there for three months, he came back before the baby was born and

then he went off trooping for two years. He was a regular soldier stationed in Wales and we lived in married quarters until 1957. We went to Tripoli, Malta, the Suez Canal in Egypt… we were evacuated in 1952. When Farouk abdicated, the first trouble started, and we had to come out. I was on the sixth plane that came out. We came out into Lyneham, Wiltshire, big airports where all the baggies come back to. My husband came back three or four months later. We went to Falmouth, to a coastguard's cottage.

"The place we had to stay in was pretty grim, after coming back from being stationed abroad. I had to go back to an oil stove, and we got our own curtains and rugs. [Now they have been transformed into luxury flats.] My husband was stationed at Penzance Castle and he had a quarter on the cliffs. We then went to Portland Dorset, moved to Germany for three years and went to Scotland for six months; that was like a holiday. My husband left the services in 1957."

What was the best thing for you about being involved?

"I had a wonderful job; half the time I was not restricted to camp, I could travel, I had a lot of freedom. It was a rather different existence from just living on a camp. I enjoyed the company. Our officers trained with us in Oxford, twelve rookie [1] officers trained with us and thirty-six WAAFs; we were all rookies, so wherever you went you knew somebody. Some of the thirty-six WAAFs became officers, it was a different atmosphere."

Any specific anecdotes?

"We worked very hard. The girls I was with were very pleasant people; I was in touch for a time, but my husband and I travelled so much, we lost touch with them. I was a founder member of the WAAF Club in Southend-on-Sea. Southend was number three of the WAAF clubs, but my husband had Alzheimer's. He was very difficult, he was not an easy person to take anywhere, he would upset people. I stopped going to WAAFs because I could not leave him on his own and I have never gone back."

[1] Newly nominated as officers

ELIZABETH CLIFTON
(NÉE PAULINE GUYFAW)

Plotter, WAAF, 1942-1945

Elizabeth lives in Northumberland, in RAF accommodation at Rothbury. She very kindly offered to collect me from Morpeth station and drive me back to her home. It is not every day that I meet a woman over eighty years old proudly holding onto her "red" walking stick and driving a Ferrari-red Fiat 500. Elizabeth is bursting with life, full of energy, and refuses to be tied down by her ailments. I was not surprised when she told me that she is a volunteer in the local police force.

We drove through beautiful countryside past Alnwick down to Rothbury, where we held our photo session at the RAF Hotel. Elizabeth left school at sixteen; her first job was working for an insurance company down in London at the Royal Exchange, then she moved down to Surrey when the war broke out.

"I left school at sixteen and was working for an insurance company. I moved from London exchange to be evacuated to Surrey and got acquainted with one of my colleagues, who told me that she was going to join the WAAF. She invited me to come with her. I said, why not?" She waited until she was able to join on the second anniversary of the Battle of Britain. "It could not have been a better day. I went to Morecambe (Lancashire) on the coast. We had to stay in a hotel where they hated us because they wanted the rooms for their guests, even though it was not the holiday season; they had to turn

out all their guests for the military. It was freezing cold, we had terrible food. One day she (the landlady) gave us this one pudding and we said it was so nice to have pudding, from there on we had sponge pudding every day! On the day we had the immunisations we were all terribly ill that night, the landlady did not find anything better than serving us cold tea cups."

Elizabeth was sent to another training camp to get a grasp of the WAAF side of it and then she was posted to a secret radar station in Hampshire, with fighter command. They were responsible for the air activity.

"This was a very small radar station. We were connected to various stations around, and we used to get fed the information from other stations. If you have seen war movies with women moving plots on a map, that is what I did. We also had the radar side, it was called 'ground control interception'. We were in touch with the pilots, they had a little radar set in their cockpit and we would direct them as near to the enemy as we could see and they would then take over. This was all terribly secret then, although it is common knowledge now. They would get the positions of the enemy and plot them on the map. Ours was more an overall picture, the radar operation would be in touch with the pilots, we would get our information fed through from fighter command stations nearby.

"You had to be so quick, we had about four or five around the table to plot, constantly connected to various stations depending on the activity. It was a grid, you had to get it exactly right, you had to do around about thirty to forty plots an hour. We had to read all this information back again to other stations to give them the grid reference. The shift was killing, absolutely killing, we'd be up again at 5 am. We only got one proper night's sleep in four, and being a small station, there was no NAAFI. We had to light the fire in the kitchen, we had to do a week in the kitchen every month. The cook we had… one day we really thought she'd got the message. We had rice pudding and we thought, oh, this is nice, then someone said, "Stop eating it! There are cockroaches in it!" They had condemned the house for the RAF and they put us in it! The cheddar cheese and the meat were brought to us in coal lorries, you had to scrape off the outside from the cheese.

"Four weeks before D-day we were put on rations; chips, biscuits, cheese and milk, that's all we had for three weeks. We were in Sopley Park [Hampshire], the Manor House. We had a room for seven, no furniture, nothing. We brought orange boxes for bedside cupboards.

"We were invited over to the American camps to present a play; when we entered the camp we saw some great buckets with some yellow liquid in them and thought what on earth is that? They said, "Grapefruit juice, help yourself." During the interval they gave us a meal, we had never seen anything like this – cold pork chops, the most gorgeous tomato sauce, fruit salad and cream, which has always been my favourite. I can remember we did ask after the break, the Americans could not believe what we had lived on. They had a Mustang and they were so useless with their servicing, the petrol tank would fall off. When I look back over D-Day, all the

Mustangs were painted with black and white stripes.

"On D-Day I saw hundreds of black and white striped planes flying over and I told my roommates, and the other six said, "Go back to sleep!" How could they miss that! This was history being made, I could not just not watch that. I was there till seven months after D-Day, then I was posted up to Trimley, near Felixstowe in Suffolk. I was there for the V1 and V2; we could see the V2s taking off from Holland and we were thinking where will they land in London?

"That was quite an interesting spot. One of my friends, Elizabeth, was slightly posh; she'd never had fish and chips, so I took her down to a fish and chip place. Her father was in the army and they moved to a penthouse flat in Park Lane where her uncle lived. Elizabeth and I were invited over for lunch and here we were, two scruffy WAAFs in this very posh place! Sadly I lost touch with her. I stayed there until the war was over. When we were demobbed, we had to go back to the original camp in Innsworth, Gloucester, and that was terrible. It was a massive, massive camp, there were only three transports for us. One girl was trampled to death because there was not enough transport. Then I had a breakdown and was sent home for three months. My GP said, 'I am not sending you back at all, or you are going to have another breakdown! You either have it now or when you are going to be demobbed!'

"I was demobbed early, having stayed three-and-a-half years instead of four. I went in September 1942 and came out December 1945. For a lot of them you had to wait your turn to be demobbed, you didn't just go after the war was finished, you had to wait your turn."

How did you apply?
"You just applied, you signed up. Obviously you had to fill in details and if they thought you weren't suitable, they would say 'sorry'. Clerk Special Duties (SD) was quite some high class trade. I was just lucky, I had no idea what the various trades were. It was just luck. I was stationed with my friend right up until I went to Trimley. The friend who signed up with me was so gorgeous, she got married while she was there; her

husband was a fighter pilot, he was shot down during the war. We stayed in contact for years and years, she was wonderful. She used to be so cross with me because I did not want to go out to dances, because I was always so tired.

"She taught me how to ride a bike – when we had a two-mile walk from the camp, they gave us bikes. I had never ridden a bike before, because my parents did not allow me. On night watch I would cycle with blankets on the handlebars. I would never have wished any different, even though the camp conditions were so harsh in Sopley.

"We had one girl, she was very old fashioned, she was nearly thirty. Some of them had never worn flat shoes in school. The shoes were lace-ups in black leather, those who had never worn flat shoes had terrible trouble with their calves. We had woollen panties, oh, the quality! And these amazing bloomers that you could pull right up to your armpits! The beds we slept on were called biscuits, three mattresses, you had to stack them. In the morning we used to sit on our biscuits and try to put holes in our stockings with the wires to get a new supply of stockings. Towards the end of the war you were allowed silk stockings if you were out, especially the officers. We used to have a jacket and skirt and then they decided to put us in battledress because of night watch, and we stayed in it."

What was the best about your time in the WAAF?
"The best was, I suppose… oh, the glamour of the uniform. The quality of the bloomers was exceptional. Volunteering was everything I applied for and I felt that it was a privilege to be in operation, to do something worthwhile. I greatly enjoyed the camaraderie and the mix of people, ladies and land girls were working next to each other. I think it was the work we were doing, I was so lucky that I was in fighter command.

"My father, who was an awful snob, wanted me to go into the WRNS and I said, 'I am not interested in ships, but I am interested in aircraft'. I did not want to go into the ATS. I thought I might be called up later on and decided that I would rather sign up early to do what I want. I was lucky with the trade the WAAF put me in. We all got on so well together as we had similar backgrounds, and we had this job in fighter command… in operation, you were in the midst of all the action. The companionship, the fact that you were doing something worthwhile, which may be an awful cliché, but I remember when I came out of the WAAF I got a job. I remember sitting on the platform thinking, we had nothing. I didn't go to dances because I had a boyfriend who was abroad. I just think, the conditions we had were not exactly luxurious, we were sent out on night duty with a loaf of bread and tea. I was so hungry. We just did it. I don't think we had the expectations in those days that they have got now."

Do you have any specific anecdotes?
"One position I had was around the big table in Tangmere [West Sussex] and this girl was passing plots to me and you could hear the bombs falling. Suddenly we heard the voices get more and more faint. I often wondered what happened to them; these stations on the South Coast were so badly bombed. My father wanted me to be an officer, the only commission I could get was in admin, but I wanted to be on the operation board. There was this song at the time, '*I want to be a clerk SD and sit on my controller's knees, oh though I know it shouldn't be, I know it's foolish but it's fun*'. I said to my parents, "At least I did not sit on my controller's knee." My father was only a private during the First World War. I said, 'You never got your stripes,' and he said, 'I did not want the responsibilities'. I said, 'Ah, shirking off the responsibility,' and I never spoke to him ever again. He was so Victorian, for him a woman's place was in the home, preferably in the kitchen. My mother said, 'She is right!'

"I did not want to go to admin. The job I got was one of choice, for a job as radar operator you needed a bit of brain. Even though the kitchen girls were nice, they did not have much education. When you were discharged you just had to go, you just got your coupons and that was it. OK, you've done your job, you can go; it was very odd, really."

ESTHER POINTON

Barrage balloon operator and
motor transport mechanic, WAAF, 1941-1945

Esther joined the WAAF in December 1941. She spent her first two years working as a barrage balloon operator; these were large balloons that were used to prevent bomber aircraft flying low and bombing in large cities like Liverpool.

"Lots of the time I was in Liverpool, it was to defend from lower-level bombing. After two years I did motor transport mechanics (MTM). I did my training just out of Blackpool and then the first posting was off to Stranraer, in Scotland. I was at a station called West Row, just outside Stranraer, for a year. Little Staughton (North Bedfordshire), was the station where I spent the last year of the war and where I met my husband."

Why did you choose to join the WAAF?
"I don't know – I think it was just the concept of flying and helping the flyers, you know? There were great posters out there, 'Serve with the men who fly'. I went straight into the WAAF; you had to pass a medical. They did not ask me what I wanted to do. I initially thought about the WRNS, but you couldn't go into the WRNS unless you had past members of your family in the navy. My next choice was the WAAF.

"I am originally from Lancashire, Rossendale Valley. I met my husband and he was from Chester, that is how I ended up in Chester. First we had to go to Innsworth, which is in Gloucestershire. We were kitted out there. Then we went to Morecambe for square-bashing and

lectures. After three or four weeks we were sent just outside Liverpool to do our balloon training. The balloon training lasted about three months. The first night of our training was in a camp, you were taught the procedure and then you went to camp side and did the work, then passed the exam. Before being posted to our balloon station, another girl and I were sent to Bradford to do a driving course, then we were sent back to Liverpool."

What did you have to do with the balloons?
"Well, you get in the winch; it was like a big lorry, it was fifteen tonnes. You could drive it like a lorry and the back was the winch. The reason we were sent on a driving course was to drive the balloons around; in case of heavy bomb attack you had to fly the balloon at a certain altitude and when the attack was over, you got a phone call telling you to let it down. There were six girls on each side and it was very dirty work, on the balloons. We received the information from the watchers."

What was your duty when you moved to the MTM?

"It was mainly repairing transport mechanics. Yes, you did move them from A to B around the site, it was mainly mechanical work and it was the first time WAAFs were used as mechanics. When we went up to Stranraer, there were two old men who could not believe they had sent WAAFs as mechanics, they hardly believed that we could do the work; they first started to ask us to clean planks until they got used to us.

"We mainly had to repair big staff lorries, Bedfords and Fords, mainly big trucks. I moved down to Bedfordshire to a bomber squadron for the same duty there as mechanics, MTM."

What would you say was best about your time in the WAAF?

"I would say the comradeship. Everybody was in the same boat, and everything was rationed, anyway. You met a lot of different people; they taught you to stand up for yourself."

Do you have any specific anecdotes about that time?

"When I was in Stranraer, this station I was on, every six weeks the bomb shifter aircrew, pilots, came and got in for night training on their log books. There were quite a few accidents; when you heard the bagpipes you knew there was a plane crash somewhere. Although it was a small station it seemed to lend itself to that, the weather was miserable up there. I remember the train journey was terrible. Me, living in Lancashire, by the time I would get home it was half past seven in the morning. There was never any heating on the trains, and only army personnel were travelling, and it was freezing.

"Often you were allowed on leave; about every three months, supposedly, you got ten days. At one time, around the build up to D-Day, our leave was stopped and I didn't get one for nearly a month. I had a friend in Glasgow and went to visit her for a couple of weekends there, which was a bit of a break."

How did your parents react?

"Well, my father did not like it one bit. I had to say to him: 'In another year they can send me to a munitions factory or anywhere they want, and this is what I want to do'. But he never liked it."

Do you know why?

"I suppose... they used to say when I joined, there were a lot of girls who joined from big cities, I suppose I was pretty naive to them because where I lived we weren't anything like that. We were a bit old fashioned, I guess my dad was scared of the influence. I could have left in the first two weeks, but chose to stay, I got used to it. My mum knew that every ten days there would be a letter. She had my brother, who was still staying at home, and the rest of the family was around. The only other brother was in the army, he was nineteen years older than me and I was the only girl. The oldest boy and the youngest girl were in the army, the rest at home, there were six of us. My brother was a dispatch rider, he was put on the boat and was in his forties.

"At the end of the war, they did not want you to stay, obviously there were too many of us there and not enough jobs for everybody to do. We were obviously taking the place of men that were sent abroad and I was doing a man's job, they did not want you to take a man's job. I got down to London to get demobbed and joined my husband, who was in the air force. My friend and I organised two reunions. We grew to over three hundred. The first one was in 1986. We've gone to one in Wales, where we met a group of ladies, some of them from the Lake District. It took us nearly a year to organise a reunion in Chester, that was so many people that we had a waiting list, we had three hundred people. Two years later we were three hundred and forty. It takes about twelve months to organise such an event. We got the Mayor to come, we had the church for ex-services, the Reverend was rubbing his eyes to see so many in the church.

"I am glad I had the experience. It does make you independent; it takes a while, though I think it was easier to blend in for girls who came from the big towns. I was quite shy and did not mix very easily, but the girl who took me under her wing came from Hull. She was an instructor for the ladies, she was three years older than me, she kind of got fond of me. She and I went on the driving course, we stayed in touch, I was her one of her bridesmaids, but then we lost touch."

You had quite a difficult job?

"They offered us different jobs because I was in group two, the highest a girl on balloon could be in. I wanted to transfer, but the sergeants, two men, tried to remaster me to special police, which was group five, which was the lowest. At the end of the training, though, they said that I would be a corporal and then made a sergeant, and that I would get the perks of being a sergeant, but I didn't want to be a military policeman; I could not do that. The redcaps, they were called, no way!"

How did they distinguish the groups? Was it by difficulty of the job?

"Funnily enough, you know, pilots went group five. I don't know how they organised the groups; group two was the only group for women on balloons. I suppose because it was a hard job, and dirty, and you had to get up in the middle of the night when there was a storm to get everything lined up. The sergeant used to say. 'You're silly, you have a dirty job, you know I have an easier one'. They stopped using the balloons 1942-43… it must have been at the end of 1943, they started taking girls off balloons and then we were remastered for 1944-45."

KATHLEEN COVE

Motor transport mechanic, WAAF, 1942-1946

Since I started this project I have met the most amazing people and have been welcomed with open arms, everybody willing to give a hand to help me out with the project. Today I went to a new region up north, to a county I had never previously set foot in: Cumbria. It took me a good four hours to travel to a wild but beautiful coast with washed-out colours and spirit-calming landscapes.

I encountered Kathleen Cove and her son, Stephen, who very kindly picked me up from the station and drove me to his mum's home. He also invited me to join them for dinner, and we had a very nice meal in an Italian restaurant in the middle of a city centre where you could still see the past splendour of a mining city. Kathleen had arranged for her son Stephen to meet me at Millom railway station. He explained that Kathleen was very anxious about being photographed and he felt she should never have called me, but it would be difficult to escape now that I was meeting her.

To put her at ease, I decided to take her portrait before the interview and looked for a suitable place. With no war monument in sight and a hefty wind, I decided to set up her portrait in Stephen's house, just next door. To me every sitter is different. I usually get to know them better when we speak about their experience as a volunteer, but with Kathleen we had little time to know each other before starting the photography. She very kindly listened to my instructions

and I felt that she wanted the session to be over as soon as possible. The picture I have chosen is one where she looks proud and is sitting tall; I would later discover that Kathleen is a very strong character and only the ailments of age would give her pause. For Kathleen, joining the WAAF was something she did based on a sense of duty.

"I joined the WAAF on my eighteenth birthday in 1942, in Bradford. It was a Saturday morning and I went into town where they recruited. I just had to sign a paper and they told me they would let me know. I went in September and went to Brentmoor for initial training. During the summer of 1942 I went on holiday with my friend's parents in St Ann's, where all the Motor Transport (MT) WAAF were training, and I thought that sounds interesting. While we were on holiday the brother of my friend was reported missing in the air force; we came back early and I came back with the idea that, yes, I did want to join the WAAF. I did not know you could join before you were eighteen and all you needed was to get your parents' permission. I wanted my friend to join as well, but she had three brothers in the air force and one of them was lost, so she did not join."

Did you say you wanted to be a driver?
No. When they interviewed me, they suggested I should be a clerk SD, and you may know that they become plotters, but I didn't know what that meant and I did not want to be a clerk. I wanted to work on aeroplanes and I joined as a flight mechanic. We had about three months' training in Hednesford (Staffordshire) near Cannock, then I was posted to a station, then to Holton, in Oxfordshire where I was trained as a fitter 2E, that's an engine fitter instead of a flight mechanic. It was the next stage – it must have been another three months. Hednesford was just a training camp. That's where I met my husband, he was in the Fleet Air Arm.

When I went to Hogan it was a police stamp service station with three-storey blocks; my husband had been there as an apprentice and I was following in his footsteps. There was an aerodrome with only a few aeroplanes at that time. I did run up to a Spitfire, sit in the plane and check the controls. You did a check list if you were posted in an active station, but going from flight mechanic to fitter 2E, I never did that. I was mostly in the big hours, where the aeroplanes flew so many hours. The planes had to have an examination and after a few more hours they had to have a major service, where they took everything to pieces. You were always told that you might have to fly in the plane you were servicing and you had better make sure you serviced it properly. I never had to do that, but some WAAFs had to. I did go on a flight one time when I was stationed at Little Rissington and I flew to Brize Norton. It probably was in an Oxford, this is the type of plane we were working on, as our station was not an active, but a flying training station. I went to Church Lawford near Rugby;

I was there for D-Day. Before D-Day we did not really know what was going on, but all leave was stopped. I got a bit depressed and applied for a transfer. I was sent to Little Rissington near Cheltenham, and at both places I was doing similar work. At Church Lawford we were in a hut with a corrugated roof, it was a horrible place, one shelf to put your things on. In Little Rissington we were billeted in what was the married airmen's quarters; there was a room upstairs and one downstairs, and there were four of us in the downstairs room. Four beds and one big cupboard, everything you'd got had to fit in there. I was lucky because the other girls there were electricians and they could get accumulators, so they could have a radio. We were able to listen to the American Forces Network. Whenever I hear any of the tunes they used to play it takes me back all over the years, to when I heard them over and over again. At home you had no idea what was going on. There were no newspapers, you did not really see it unless you went in the NAAFI, it was a very enclosed situation, really. You were not part of what was going on in the bombed places. The instructors put my name forward to become an educational and vocational teacher (EVT) in Catterick (Yorkshire), and I taught geography, economics, and helped with the education of army servants. I was made a sergeant and got the opportunity to learn to drive. I was eligible for discharge in 1946, when I got married; my husband was based in Sri Lanka for a few months and later we moved to Cornwall.

How did your parents react?
(Kathleen giggles.) "It was funny, I just had an older sister and my mother was convinced she made me join, but it wasn't the case. She eventually joined later, she was sent to munitions which she absolutely hated, and then decided to volunteer in the Land Army."

When I asked Kathleen about the best she remembers of her experience as a WAAF, she said, 'It was all about having a good time'. Her memory about this time is very positive, she is grateful for the opportunity for what she could learn in the air force, it was an experience that taught her something. I was not surprised when Kathleen told me, 'Because I missed going to university during the war, I decided to study for a BA at sixty-four!'

Being someone who knew exactly what it meant to be a volunteer, she wrote her dissertation about the women who volunteered during WWII. The funny thing was that her lecturer asked her if she thought she would be able to finish her BA, starting at such an advanced age; I don't know if this lecturer is still alive, but Kathleen is still going strong.

JANE ELDRIGE

Cipher officer, WRNS 1941-1945

Jane was one of the first volunteers I met. She lives in a retirement flat for ex-naval officers near the Naval Academy in Greenwich, London, and she very kindly welcomed me into her new home, then took out her photo albums and the documents she had collected from her time in the services. Jane served in the WRNS as a cipher officer, decrypting important messages. The WRNS was one of the few women's services that allowed women to work and travel on troopships. Jane sailed on the Queen Mary and HMS Renown when Churchill and his Chief of Staff were on board, travelling to war conferences in Alexandria and Quebec. The code name to send her on mission on ship was 'monster'.

She told me: "I had always thought it meant, you know, the Admiralty thought it was monstrous that women should go to sea, but I learned afterwards it was simply an indication that 'monster' was a troopship, because the Queen Mary and most of the ships were very big and took thousands of troops on board."

If women were admitted on troopships it was because they needed them to decipher the secret messages, which would allow the naval officers to keep in action. I met Jane for a few photo sessions until we found the right place to take her portrait; at some point we were allowed to take a portrait of her in the naval chapel at the Naval Academy in Greenwich, which was set aside for an hour for the shoot before opening to the public. Jane has been extremely patient, devoting a lot of time to these sessions and putting a lot of energy into it.

WINIFRED ARMSTRONG

Motor transport driver, WAAF, 1942-1945

Winifred recently celebrated her ninetieth birthday and is very mobile, often getting out and about. She lives in a leafy suburb near Leicester and still occupies the house where she stayed with her husband after coming back from Australia; she lived in Melbourne for twenty-seven years. "We went out with my husband on those £10 single tickets you could get at the time. I could not have stayed at home. She used to work as a pharmacist for Beecham in Melbourne and volunteered for twenty years in an Oxfam shop.

She had to come back to Leicester after her husband had a stroke and I felt that this was not her first choice, but it did not stop her from living her life. If Winifred decided to join the WAAF, it was because of her boyfriend; he was in the RAF and she sensed that it was something she wanted to do as well. She was twenty in June 1942 and started her training in Innsworth with the traditional 'square-bashing'.

[At the huts] there was a sergeant and she came around and kissed us all good night and we thought, isn't that nice of her? Later we got to learn that she was a lesbian, we were all that innocent! It was June and boiling hot, we were all in uniform and we had to listen to the commanders and officers; several of the girls fainted and we were not allowed to pick them up! It was very difficult to stand there indeed. I was sent to Wheaton near Blackpool to train as a station driver, although I spent my first weeks in the kitchen because there were no instructors available.

"Driving was always something I wanted to learn to do and I liked it. It was difficult, I was half an inch too short, I was only five foot two and something and you needed to be five foot three to be a driver.

"My recruitment papers got mixed up and I managed to do the test to be a driver. I passed, with very good marks, and the officer said, "Would you rather be an MT driver instead of an operator?" I said, "Oh, yes!" She put me forward, explaining that even though I was too short, I was good enough to drive. I was then moved after ten weeks' training and went up a rank. Because I love driving, I suppose I was good at it. I use to drive at six o'clock in the morning with the milkman – not the electric milk floats, but an ordinary lorry. This helped me move up a rank and driving was really something I enjoyed.

"I went to Pwllheli in North Wales to do a driving course, we had an amount of time on cars and six weeks on lorries. It was very hilly; the test was in a lorry, I had to double declutch to change gears. The instructor would put a matchbox behind the wheel and you had to drive this lorry up the steep hill without crushing the matchbox. I used to drive three-ton lorries, and cars,

driving officers and crew around the airfield. The longest distance I drove was from Oxford to Newcastle. As a lorry driver, in harsh winter, we girls had to crawl under the lorry to drain the water out of the heating system to avoid freezing, as there was no anti-freeze available. Because there was no transport anywhere we used to hitch rides; you would not think about it these days, but we would just go out onto the main road and hitch, and nobody had any troubles. We were about twenty girls in the hut, your bed had to be unmade every morning, every blanket, and look neat and tidy.

"At the time of the bombing in London, we used to go to London on leave – we used to get a week's leave every three months. We were on duty forty-eight hours in a row. I was on night duty when, during my twenty-first birthday, everybody was hiding mugs [of cider or beer] under the table when the officer came round. My next posting was Cottesmore, but it was closed down. The Americans took over and built a new aerodrome at Market Harborough. I was sent to Market Harborough, but I would have preferred to be sent abroad, although women were not allowed to carry arms at the time. We

were bombed while there and we got some new lorries out of that. We were billeted in a big house, the painter Gainsborough had lived there. While I was there I used to drive all sorts of vehicles. My duty was to drive whenever they needed me, whether it was for an ambulance or anything else. It was a great life, we were driving big lorries, taking the crews out, and it was a training aerodrome for crew and bomber pilots.

"My time there was not plain sailing, though; because this was a training airfield, I witnessed a few air disasters, there is a sad story attached to that. As drivers, we had come from Cottesmore to Market Harborough, about ten miles, because we carried everything over in transport. The first day we were there, we stood at the end of the runway, they used to have empty huts at the end of the runway, and there were six guys in a lorry. I think they were going home as they'd just finished, and just as they went across the runway, a plane from Cottesmore came in to land and hit them, and all of them were killed. Our first job was to pick all those bodies up. These lads were only eighteen, nineteen and twenty years old, we used to take them out to the planes,

Before dawn on the 9th of April 1945 several "W.A A.F. M. T. Drivers were sleeping in a Nissan hut (Named Admin View!) on a W. A. A. F. site near FOXTON – part of "14 O. T. U." MARKET HARBOROUGH, LEICESTERSHIRE.
I was one of them! We were awakened by the sound of a LANCASTER BOMBER – obviously in trouble, we arose, put on the hut light, forgetting the "Blackout", rushed to the door of the hut to see the LANCASTER heading straight for the hut – WE ALL WERE PETRIFIED and not one of us could move to try to save ourselves. The "NOSE" of the LANCASTER rose slightly and it crashed in a field near Foxton, just a few hundred yards away from our hut. Sadly all the crew were killed.
We were all convinced that the pilot had seen the light from our hut and managed to lift the LANCASTER slightly and so save all our lives!!

Winifred Elizabeth Armstrong (Nee HEAWOOD)
L.A.C.W. W.A.A.F. M. T. DRIVER 1942 to 1946

see them off and some of them never returned, because there was a hill at the end of the runway. Also the parents would come and ask if we would have been able to see their son. It all was a dreadful experience picking up those dead bodies and not allowing their family to see them because some of them were separated in body parts. We knew that none of them were whole but were not allowed to say anything. That was dreadful, driving slowly at the back of the hearse and having their parents there. It was a job to be done, despite the tough experience."

This was the most excruciating experience for Winifred, 'seeing all these young lads off to fly and not see them coming back'.

How did you parents react when you joined?

"My mother was fuming because I volunteered, and my father took me aside, he'd lost his right arm in the First World War, and he said, 'Don't take any notice of her, I am proud, my sons aren't old enough to go, I am so glad you volunteered'. That was very nice of him, but perhaps he only wanted to get rid of me!"

What would you say was the best about your experience in the WAAF?

"I would say, you mixed with people of all stations in life, we had a lady who was an MT driver, the comradeship, everybody pulled together, because we were all volunteers we weren't made to go."

What Winifred enjoyed most about her time in the WAAF was the mix of people, the comradeship. There were no class issues and everybody was hands on. Because they chose to be volunteers, everybody was treated the same. It seems that flying was always a wish for Winifred and guess how she celebrated her ninetieth birthday? She went up in a glider, of course. Who said life is over at eighty? Not for some, that's for sure. Winifred is an amazing lady.

Winifred celebrated her 90th birthday in style by flying in a glider

MARY ELLIS

Pilot, Air Transport Auxiliary, 1941-1946

Mary joined the ATA in 1941. She had an interest in aeroplanes long before that and already had a pilot's licence. When the war started she was flying private planes, which made her wonder if it meant the end of her flying when the war started, though new flying opportunities opened up for her when she was accepted in the ATA.

How did you find out about the ATA? Did they put out an advertisement?

"Yes, somewhere. I found out about them because I listened to the wireless [the radio]; they were asking for anyone with a pilot's licence to contact them. I thought, could I do it? I said to my mother, "I think I will apply." My father was more against it as he was concerned about me getting involved in the war. I applied and they invited me for an interview, and fortunately they were pleased with me and I was accepted. We were billeted with families and civilians, we had the best of two worlds, as it could be said. We had cars to go to the airfield from 9 am to 9-10 pm. We did not have to do a certain number of flying hours, we had to be there every day for a fortnight, then we had to have two days' leave, whether we wanted it or not; most of us wanted to fly all the time. It did not matter about the hours, you had to be on duty, although if the weather was really bad, you were dismissed for the day. There was no night time flying, there was a night duty for two of us to take in the

programme via the telephone for all the aeroplanes that had to be moved to secret places. It was easier to fly every day than every six months.

"An ATA was flying mostly alone, sometimes with an engineer if there was an emergency. It was so interesting, you were not allowed to have any contact with the ground at all. No aids, only the mechanical instruments. They did not tell us at which level we had to fly, but the control tower must have known how to handle each person, because there were different aeroplanes in different places. It really was wonderful, because of the training I had the opportunity to fly different types of aircraft. I moved around quite a lot. After training on single engines, I was posted to number 15 pool in Hamble and stayed there. Our training was supposed to be two years and it was cramped into three months." She shows me a picture of her in front of a huge aircraft (picture on next page). "They did not have much time for training. Hamble closed and I was posted to number 6 pool in Huckley, which closed as well, and I was then posted elsewhere. I was probably the last one left, most of them had already left in 1945." She shows me the book *Forgotten Pilots: a Story of the Air Transport Auxiliary,* by Lettice Curtis [1]

"We were flying from A to B and had to find out where to land. Sometimes you followed the railways to find your way, but then they took off the name of railway stations, which made it impossible. There was no such thing as a flight plan, there was this piece of paper. I left Hamble and I was completely on my own after take-off. One was never forced to fly, if you thought the weather was not good enough, you did not. There was the take-off, we did not know where to go, we knew where we should deliver the aeroplane to, but we had no direction: we would use the compass and a map, and draw a line on the map." She shows me one of her flying maps, which is completely falling apart from extensive use. See picture page 39.

"After a while, at about seventy miles from Hamble, all the landmarks were camouflaged, which made it difficult to follow your way on the map at 200 miles an

hour. One day when I took off there was a thick haze and I could not see; we had to fly in a formation, I just managed to see out of the mist and followed the circuit in preparation for landing, but as I touched down another aeroplane came on to the same runway; it was a near miss. She had not seen me, I had not seen her, we made a mistake that day, there was no one to tell us we were that close.

"I had one or two forced landings. While I was over the New Forest, my engine stopped. Nobody can stay up for very long when this happens and there was not much empty space in the New Forest, but fortunately I found one; this was with a Spitfire, as you know the undercarriage was very low, and I crash-landed. It was all right at the time as I did not really realise the risk it was, only afterwards. We had to have parachutes, but never learned to jump. Some of the aircrafts had bucket seats with the parachute inside, which we sat on, and safety belts [Sutton Harness] from the aircraft. I did not like wearing helmets at all, it felt quite safe anyway. We did not have to take any officials, but occasionally we had to pick up someone from where he lived.

Mary flew about four hundred Spitfires and other

[1] English woman aviator, flight test engineer, air racing pilot, she became one of the first women to join the ATA.

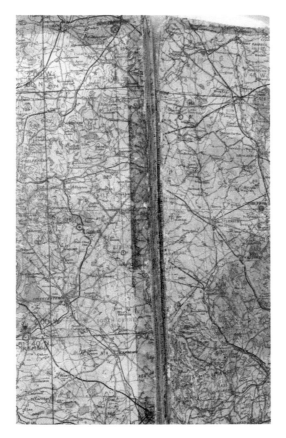

military aircraft. Hers is an amazing story; she became a private pilot after the war. She knew a man from the Isle of Wight who had a farm on the island and another near Gatwick. He wanted to go back and forth between them quickly, so she used to fly him where he wanted to go and did that for years. After flying all these commercial aeroplanes, women were still not allowed to become pilots, it was a different life. She then operated the Isle of Wight airfield, which accepted holiday flights in Dakota aircraft from Exeter, Leeds, and Manchester. The owner of the airfield offered her the position of manager; at that time Sandown Airport had as many landings as London Airport. Mary was married in 1961 to a pilot who "married the airport boss".

"Out of the women ATA pilots stationed in Humble there are four left today: Joy [Joy Lofthouse, see p. 1], Mary, Molly and Margaret." She shows me a badge she got as an award for her years in service. "We got an award, which was a great honour, and it was lovely to get recognition. There was nothing after the war; it was only a couple of years ago we were invited to 10 Downing Street."

What was the best aspect of it?
"We were absolutely privileged to be able to fly these wonderful aeroplanes, from Tiger Moths to jets, which was fantastic. We sometimes flew four different types of aircraft in a day, it was marvellous, but it had to stop; we did not want the war to go on. Once when I stepped off the ladder having climbed down from an aircraft with my parachute on my back, I was asked, "Where is the pilot?" I said, "I am the pilot!" They did not believe me, to the point where that they searched the aircraft! I said, "No, there is nobody in there." I can still see their astonished faces!

"I flew bombers on my own. We often met bomber pilots in the mess and one morning I asked, "What's happened this morning?" Grim-faced, they replied, "They did not come back." There was a high price to pay, of course. I lost several friends, there was a war and everybody was doing their bit. I met Joy [Lofthouse] not long before they closed Hamble; she was so beautiful. If the weather was bad there was no flying for a couple of hours, then there was a mad rush to get our things once we were allowed in the air again. Fifty per cent out of the training school did not make it, it was a challenge to learn everything in three months. There was a wonderful comradeship in Hamble. There is a big hospital; we went there to see the soldiers and they were so pleased to see us. I left the ATA six months after the end of the war, in 1946."

DIANA LINDO

Motor transport driver, WAAF, 1941-1946

Before the war started, Diana was living in Portugal. She was in school in the UK until the summer holidays of 1939; the school did not reopen in September. Her dad wanted her to move to America, but finally agreed she could join her aunt in Portugal. She moved back to England early July of 1941, flew over with KLM to Bristol then and took a train to London to stay with her aunt in Surrey. She remembers how difficult it was to know where to get off the train, as all the station names had been taken down.

She registered with the Air Ministry on August 4th and was called to enrol in the WAAF on October 13th. She started with the regular square-bashing introduction to learn about rules and regulations over four weeks and was then sent to North Wales to be taught driving, in cars, lorries and vans. Her first station was in Gloucestershire; she stayed there for six months then was moved to a Polish bomber station in Lincolnshire. Diana had already learned to drive when she was eighteen, in Portugal; her aunt's chauffeur taught her secretly because she was still under age – you had to be twenty-one to obtain a regular licence. She quite enjoyed her time in Lincolnshire and was later moved to the barrage balloon headquarters in London, driving officers to all the sites to be inspected.

She remembers the V2s falling on to East London, telling me, "They didn't make any noise before reaching their target, they just dived and banged." In May 1945 she was stationed in a fighter group in Uxbridge and was demobbed in May 1946. She then moved back to Portugal to get married; unfortunately her husband died eight months later and she was left on her own with a daughter. She moved back to the UK in 1950 to remarry and had a son.

Diana has published a book about her time in the WAAF, 'Wartime jottings about a WAAF driver at war, 1941-45".

DOROTHEA ABBOTT

Land Army, 1942-1946

At ninety-two, Dorothea lives on her own in a flat. She still gets out and about. She knew she was likely to be called up and decided to join the Land Army in 1942 rather than being picked up to work in a factory. She had to register because she was over twenty-one in 1941, and preferred to choose something between land and nursing. She worked on a poultry farm on her own, there was not enough work for two and there was not much going on in the village, either. They were divided up into different counties. There was no training, her friend got one month's training at a mental hospital where they had large enough grounds to grow vegetables, and learned to use a pitchfork. She left the library where she worked on the Friday, then on Monday she travelled down to Purton (Wiltshire) and started at a farm on the Tuesday.

"I did not even know how to use a pitchfork. There was not much going on on the poultry farm, it felt quite lonely and I did not have much contact with the farmer, either. She shows me a picture where she is in uniform (above). She looks quite smart in the Land Army uniform, which was corduroy trousers, emerald green jumper and a donkey-grey coloured coat and hat; "It was only for going out, the girls would not wear the uniform for work." They had to work about eight hours a day with one weekend every month off, and got either a fortnight's leave or a week every three months, she can't quite remember.

Were you working for a specific farmer?
"When I was at the hostel there were twenty-five other girls, they were all from Birmingham, one from Solihull. We would go out every day to a different farm and see the farmer, who told us what to do. The farmers did not think much of us at first; one old man said to me, 'We are not helped with maids doing men's work'. When I was at the hostel we had to do a lot of threshing corn. They had not been able to have a machine in Warwickshire to thresh the corn, there were lots of lots of rigs that needed threshing and it needed about six or eight people all doing different jobs. When I was at the hostel it was mostly that, or muck-spreading sometimes, to fertilize the land. When I was at the poultry farm in the winter we had to grease the wood to stop the bugs crawling up and keep the hen house watertight. I used to sit in the food stores mending sacks; not very interesting, really! But I could always find something to

do. We had more to do in the summertime, the hens were a nightmare to put back into their houses then, because it was still quite light until ten o'clock, as we had double summertime then.

"I think that hens are very stupid creatures, but I did not mind the ducks and the geese; you could shepherd them, you can't do that with hens!" She looks around for pictures of the hostel she stayed in Warwickshire, adding, when she shows them to me, "When you get to my age, you can't find anything."

How did your parents react?

"They knew it was impossible not to join. They were sorry not to have me at home, but I went home every months to see them." The best thing about the Land Army was the opportunity she was given to do something different in her life. She explained that she would never have had a chance to experience something different without this opportunity. She loved the time when she was in Devon and was able to drive a motorcycle, a little Honda scooter that she used to drive around Cornwall for the weekend, which was very nice. She went from Warwickshire to Devon until she was

demobbed and went back to the library. Dorothea has written a play [1] about her time in the Land Army which has been performed on stage twice in public.

[1] Plenty of Mud by Dorothea Abbott

NANCY COOPER

Land Army, 1943 to 1950

Nancy volunteered to join the Land Army; she first tried to get in when she was sixteen but she was too young.

Why did you choose the Land Army?

"I loved this sort of life; being outside, looking after animals particularly, and eventually I joined in May 1943. I wanted to avoid the winter, I was seventeen and a half at the time. I was very fortunate because a lot of the girls in the Land Army had to start with three weeks' training. I went to Northamptonshire, to an agricultural college called Moulton College, and I went in because it was what I wanted to do and I immensely enjoyed it. I was brought up in suburban Birmingham, not exactly in the countryside.

"The cows did not frighten me at all. They could be a bit fidgety and some of the girls were frightened, and then there was me showing off. At the end of it, after four weeks' training, we were all assessed and they kept me on an extra week to help the staff, because I was good at my job and they needed my help for a fresh intake that was coming in. I only had three weeks' training to learn how to feed the animals, poultry and this sort of thing.

"In the evening we would have lectures, we had a big barn and we would sit on big bales of straw. I was a very naive girl and found out quite a lot about farming. I did not realise to get milk from the cows you needed them to have a calf first. After the training I was sent to a

place in Rugby called Barby Road, where they had very, very large houses with grounds. In these places most of the produce went to the house, which I did not like. I stayed for quite some time, around five or six months. I decided that I did not join the Land Army for this, I wanted to be on a farm; I complained and was moved.

We had to stay in our own county, which was Warwickshire. The next one was a place called Studley, a place famous for needle-making, and that was totally different. I had to be billeted out into private houses and the farmer was a dealer so he bought cows to sell them, you did not know your cows at all. They were a very nice family, it was like a second home to me; their farm was beautiful and at the back of a place called Cotton Court. There was no electricity, just lovely wood and log fires, which I loved; they used oil lamps in the evening." She explains that she wrote a poem about the place. She had a problem being billeted into soldiers' living

quarters, because the anti-social hours meant she had to leave late at night and then get back early in the morning to milk the cows, dirty and covered in muck, which was not very nice for the housewife were she was staying. She tried three different places, and had to move eventually. Because of her friends she did not want to move too far away, and she wanted to work and live on a farm, she went to Alcester, still able to see her friends. She lived on a farm which still had no electricity, milking cows.

"They used to pump the water for drinking, you had to pump for a long time, your arms nearly dropped before you could have a sip of water! That was all hand milking which was nice because you were close to your animals. I looked after twenty-two cows. We divided the work, so one day I did the whole lot of them because everybody was out in the fields.

"Double summer time meant we had to work later at night, they just told us, 'You're working tonight,' but with cows to milk in the morning it meant you had to

get up a just a few hours later. They had very strict rules in the Land Army, you were supposed to be back at your room by ten o'clock at night and when we finished work in summer after double summer time it was nearly eleven sometimes, when we were back in. You see I did not mind that at all!

"I stayed on this farm for about eighteen months until 1945, when I decided it was time to have a change. They were advertising for relief milkers, which meant that you went to different farms to help people with whatever they needed you for, if they were short of somebody. The first one they put me on - obviously my boss did not liaise with either the Land Army or anyone else, and he should have liaised with the Land Army, because they had certain things on record from other Land Girls… the farmer had some problems with sexual encounters with previous girls from the Land Army. When I was living in, he started his little tricks again! He was very soon reported by me.

"I went to various farms helping out. First of all I decided on something that could not be done and it nearly killed me doing it! They had set up a rota where they stationed me in hostels, which was quite nice for me, to be with the girls, and set my week up like Monday on one farm, Tuesday another farm, Wednesday another farm on so on for five days. They were all scattered around and some were quite far apart, with a long distance to cycle between them, and I started at five in the morning. It did not work, because the cows were all different stages and I was not given enough time to get to know them; you can't just walk in and do that. I really had to give it up because of the distance getting there - sometimes I went on duty for ten hours because I could not come back to the hostel. It was too far, I needed a rest in between; it was very difficult being on a farm.

"I ended up on one farm because the farmer had a broken leg, he'd been kicked by a cow. I was going to take on this unruly herd which I did it for quite a long time; it was a very big farm. I had to go on horseback to get the cows in and then milk them, and in the morning I had to take the milk to the milk lorries. I managed thirty cows on my own. I went back quite recently and they have not got cows any more.

"The winter of 1947 was the worst. I was still milking cows in Stratford on Avon. The farmhouse was a three-quarters of a mile drive away, an old mill going back centuries. I was on my own there and got stuck down there in the snow. It was not very nice living in, the snow was blizzarding and in the morning I had to dig my way out to the cows. Because of the weather the milking machine did not really work. The farmer did not really know much about it; he wanted to take the cows out in deep frost, when they could have broken their legs. The landlady was not very nice either because we as Land Army had a ration of cheese, but the farmers did not get it, I don't know why. She used to say to me, "I don't know why farmers don't get it and these labourers do!" It was hard to stomach, for her to hear that.

"The drive was three-quarters of a mile long and

we still had prisoners of war working on farms, and they came to dig us out; that was 1947. They came and worked with us on the farm, some stayed and did not go back, they married local girls, they were treated well. I was so pleased to get out of that place, we still had lots of snow around. The little hostel I was staying at closed down, there were only twelve of us.

"I did not know what I wanted to do next so I decided to apply to go to Devon. I came off milking, it was about time I had weekends on rest. I went to a place called Okehampton, near Dartmoor in the middle of Devon, and worked on the fields with others. I was billeted in a hostel, that was great, it felt like a holiday to me. It was very tough, really, milking cows, but I enjoyed it; it did not really feel like work!

"I stayed for a year then went back to Warwickshire, to a place called Salford Priors, as the small hostel closed. There were seventy of us and that was the end of the Land Army in 1950. I did not have a gentleman friend to tie me up, I got a ticket for a final ball at the big hostel in Priors. Then I did not know what to do and decided to go to Australia – it was ten pounds – and stayed there for three years. My mum had a business, she knew that was what I wanted to do, and she was a bit upset about me going to Australia. They found me a job in the Post Office. I stayed in a hostel there, at the Lady Musgrave Lodge, which they had taken down unfortunately. Again, I had a marvellous time there, I had promised my mother I would only stay for two years and stayed three! I intended to go back again, which I did not because I became ill.

"What I enjoyed most of all was being out in the fresh air, and the countryside – at that time you had meadows with wild flowers – all that was absolutely fantastic." (She wrote a poem about about it, next page). "Being billeted out was the worst experience; you had to go into so many private houses and they did not like you because you came back covered in muck, it was good for neither for us, imagine coming home at 11 o'clock with all these seeds in my hair! It upset them and me.

Women's Land Army

Thinking of it now seems incredible to me

Am I that same person who joined up in 1943?

Not the ATA, WAAF, or WRNS with their uniform so smart

But a very special service that was nearer to my heart.

Yes, we're an army, given a number, a badge and uniformed

But no comparison with the others were the duties we performed.

Our job was to help feed a nation whose food supply was short

We took over the jobs whilst the men went away and fought

Coming from a town needed an adjustment in many, many, ways

The work was hard, the hour long and my body ached for days

After serving in a shop things were very different now

And suddenly I was faced with washing and milking a cow!

To my surprise, with capable hands, I managed very well

I was confident in this work, no doubt, I would excel

Cows tails whipping round my head make we want to cry

Then cheeky kids come and watch, so you squirt them in the eye!

The cow muck is sloppy and splashes everywhere

Don't stand in this firing line, one cough, you'll get a share!

Milking is a seven-day job, so weekends off were few

So we had to be dedicated from that point of view

Problems were varied and had to be overcome

One of mine was related to stuff from the cows b—!

The smell of muck and milk permeate my clothes

Landladies don't like it, it offends their nose

I can't say I blame them, it wasn't very nice

No washing machines then to do the wash within a trice

So I move where I can live upon the farm

The smell doesn't matter now, so I became more calm

Out in all weathers with various jobs to do

Feeding pigs, harvesting, threshing, to mention just a few

Then there was double summer time when we finished very late

But on reflection, I loved the job, the outdoor life was great

Nobody needs a million pound to feel like a millionaire

When doing a satisfying job in the countryside pure air

The country is different now it's opened too much

No hiding place for wildlife, with developments motorways and such

No cosy little fields with hedges all around

Or varieties of wild flowers where many birds abound

So thinking about it now, it still seems incredible to me

How fortunate I was to be a member of the WOMEN'S LAND ARMY.

Nancy Cooper

RUTH BOURNE

WRNS, Bletchley Park, 1944-1946

Ruth was stationed at Bletchley Park from 1944. She was just eighteen when she joined and under eighteen when she volunteered. It was the time when the second front was being opened and she chose to volunteer because she was keen to do her bit. A lot of her relatives were in the Holocaust and she wanted to see the Germans defeated. She volunteered three times for the WRNS and was first turned down because she was only sixteen.

"After the swearing in, we were told the pay would be poor, there would be little prospect of promotion, we would work anti-social hours and, once we were accepted, we could not leave. I got into Bletchley because I had learned French, German and Spanish; at school, linguists were very much in favour in those days. I was even thrown in the deep end when I was evacuated and had to learn Welsh; none of these I got to use, but this was how I got chosen.

"I was quite terrified when I first saw the bombe machine; all these drums going round and round, I didn't know where to begin. But we had a month of training – two weeks of just watching and two weeks of hands–on experience, being watched – and then we were on our own. I was quite happy being let into the secret. I was at the station when the atomic bomb was dropped. My function then was not a bombe operator, but as I call it now, a "bombe destroyer". We had to dismantle the Turing bombe machine down to the very last wires and put all these pieces in little bits of paper, wrap them up, put them into cardboard boxes and they were sold off as army surplus.

"I was not allowed to tell my family about my role at Bletchley Park until the 1970s, as I was bound by the Official Secrets Act. There was absolute secrecy surrounding our work. When we were trained, we were told not to ask questions; do what you're told, do this, that and the other, and don't ask why. The only thing we were told was that it was one of the most secret machines in the whole war, which filled us with awe and respect. We never heard the word "Enigma" mentioned. We didn't know why there were three drums, why there was a set of drums that didn't work, why we were plugging these things in, we didn't know about the menu."

Ruth continues to volunteer as a guide at Bletchley Park; for her it is important to keep spreading the word about the Bletchley Park story. She has given talks in schools.

"Children have somewhat garbled ideas sometimes. One little boy at a school near Milton Keynes said, 'We know all about Colossus. The ladies there worked naked.' The deal was that if it got very hot and there were no engineers around, they would take off a lot of their outer garments. Wrens operating the bombes were only allowed to roll up their shirt sleeves. On night shifts they could wear what was known as 'square rig': a virtually sleeveless cotton top, with bell bottomed trousers."

PAULINE BURKE, PAM GOODGER, NORA MCMINN, LIZ DIACON

"The Warminster Volunteers"
WAAF and WRNS, 1941-1945

One evening I received a phone call from a lady called Pam Goodger. She introduced herself as an ex-WAAF and said she had seen my ad in the *RAF Magazine*. She was very keen to meet me with her three other veteran friends, who were all living very close to each other. She joked, "So you have really been dealing with geriatrics... 353 years in all!"

I took the train to Warminster Station on a very dull Wednesday morning to join them for tea. We walked to Pam's house, a lovely little cottage, where she introduced me to Nora McMinn, Pauline Burke and Liz Diacon. Pam had also invited two local journalists, one from the *Warminster Journal* and Will Frampton from the *Wiltshire Times*, ready to make this event memorable.

Pauline Burke and **Nora McMinn** served in the WRNS at Bletchley Park, where their work remained secret until 1972. "Nora and I have been neighbours for a long time, but only found out we worked virtually next door at Bletchley Park about three years ago" said Pauline. "It was such a big place you never knew what was going on and no one would tell you anything. We had to wait until thirty years after the war to find out the relevance of what we were doing."

Liz Diacon was studying at university for a degree in fine art when she joined the WAAF in June 1941, at Hornchurch. She worked with signals and remembers the good fun of taking part. Pauline joined with her sister and was stationed in Windsor between 1941–1944. She chose to join her sister, who was stationed in Bristol, during the blitz; all the stations were then moved to Windsor, where she was posted at the dispatch offices. "Life was good, with lots of entertainment," she said. "It was also a way to get away from Mum and develop good friendships."

She left the services in 1944 to marry a Wiltshire farmer, and had five children. Of her experience, she said that it was almost like finishing school: "'I learned an awful lot.'"

Nora McMinn is originally from Italy and was stationed at Bletchley Park from 1943. She joined because she wanted to be part of something; the German skills that she learned at school were a useful tool for message deciphering and finding the right words to translate the German messages. After the war she married an air force officer and travelled around the world. She really felt that she was doing a worthwhile job and met very interesting people.

Pam Goodger had served in the WAAF as a driver, towing bombs, before being promoted to catering officer. Her father was a very good driver and nothing could make her more happy than driving, she was besotted with it. She learned to drive three-tonne lorries on the hills of North Wales, and she only stopped driving when she was well into her eighties. She was very glad to have joined as a volunteer and felt that she was doing something worthwhile and constructive. "It was a training for life," she said, "and it made us independent women." They all felt immensely patriotic and wanted to do something for their country. "There was such a strong team spirit." They joined the services as soon as they were eighteen and they are now all ninety.

BERYL E ESCOTT

Author of books about women
who served in the WAAF and SOE

Beryl was not a volunteer during WWII, but joined the RAF much later, in 1961. I wanted to meet her for this project because of her knowledge and the research she had done for the book she wrote about the heroines of the Special Operations Executive service (SOE). I did not have the opportunity to meet any women who had joined the SOE and wanted to get a better insight into the role of these women through the voice of an "expert".

I began by asking Beryl if she knew of women who had joined the SOE as agents for section F (France) who were still alive today. She suggested that one of the Nearne sisters still might be living in South Africa, but after doing some research, I found that Eileen Nearne, who was part of SOE, had died in September 2010.

To be honest, I sometimes wonder where my fascination with these women comes from. Were they, as is often said, heroines? Or did they just do their job without realising the risk they were taking? Discovering that four women agents had died at the Struthof, close to where I grew up, intensified my interest. Beryl told me about the role of Vera Atkins, who was on a constant hunt to track down the men and women who were sent to France and never came back; she wanted to know what had happened to them.

"She had a thorough job, to track down people in concentration camps; she was really good, she got more information than anyone else would have got and the Germans at that time would have been keeping very good records. There was this - I can't really pronounce it, 'fog and night'." (*Nacht und Nebel.*) Some documents had unfortunately got lost.

Vera Atkins managed to track down 117 men and women, leaving only 10 or 12 who could not be traced; she also investigated other people who had been in the same camp, as prisoners there. "She was very good, only had a year to do it, was on her own and was nominally made a squadron leader. The reason she got the rank was to give her the ability to interview some of these high-ranking German officers, who would not even bother with her unless she was able to show she was of similar rank."

What triggered you to write a book about the women in SOE?

"The last book about the heroines of the SOE - it is something that always ignited me, mainly because of what some of the men had done during the war working for SOE. The SOE was a sabotage organisation and they were there to train the Resistance to be able to sabotage the right areas, factories, places where they might have munitions and various things they used. They were doing this under guidance, because normally the women were the couriers or the wireless operators. It was the most dangerous job; they had to be in contact with London, it was where their main listening station was, then they had to say, you know, what they had found. Because many of them mixed with the ordinary population, nobody should have known that they were anything different or they would be picked up by the Gestapo.

"The advantage at the beginning was that as women they would not raise suspicions and the ones sent to France were French, they had a mixed background, they could pretty well speak the language fluently so they were not hunted down as spies. They had to be pretty well perfect in their background and language, the way they would express things. They had mixed with the French they were working with, and this was very dangerous. It was inevitable that people would speak with children, or have grandparents around, and trying to keep it secret was not an easy issue and as you know the French like to talk, so they had to be on the alert all the time, and be very careful. When I came to do this, I used the book written by Professor Foot. [1]

"I spoke to him a few times about his book, *SOE in France*. This account of the work of the British Special Operation Executive in France 1940-1944 (published in 1966) was my bible. I bumped into this man in the lift when I was doing research about the WAAF in London. I went to the Imperial War Museum to do my research and was working with RAF archives. Professor Foot was asked by our government after the war to write about the history of SOE in France before everybody forgot. This was after he came out of the RAF; he was a historian before he went into the service. Anyway, he was asked by the Ministry of Defence (MOD) because he had been involved in the defence part of the government, dealing with these rather odd groups like SOE that were not even known about by the general public. People working for the SOE never heard that name until after the war, and in many cases when they were working for the organisation they called it 'the Org' and 'the Firm', because they did not have a name for it.

"The thing that annoys me most is when they are talking about the people, the women, who had been in SOE. They have always been considered spies and lots still speak about them as spies, but if you read any articles like that in the newspaper you know that the newspapers had not done sufficient research, or they would have known that SOE were never spies. These women in most cases were wireless operators, so they had to get a lot of information from and to London. In the area they were working inevitably information was collected, but it was not for that purpose; it happens that it was just useful for some other case. They were directing agents, whom they told who they should be meeting, what they should be doing and you know they need to know how to carry out their job, because it was sabotage. That also meant that they had to send messages back and forth, because they had a Resistance group.

"There were fifty to sixty Resistance groups that we know of. The Communists were the most dangerous ones and worked very well, but often would not take orders from our side. They proved to be extremely good 'résistants'. There were other parties, such as the Gaullists, and in several cases you would find that their allegiance was not to their government, not to de Gaulle either, it was to the other generals, and in fact some of the agents nearly gave up because French Resistance were not always eager to follow the information or instructions that would be forthcoming.

"The most important part of the SOE was the wireless operators; without them, you were helpless. Even if you had your little Resistance group, you had to be armed and be able to get the arms from somewhere across the Channel, and then you had to tell the RAF, who were the only ones who could bring it across easily.

They did have one or two brought in via speedboats or submarines, but not very often because they were easily spotted by the Germans, so really they had to rely on the air force and, as you know, there was a special group formed, very much against the will of Bomber Harris, as we called him, because they were some of his best pilots.

"They used RAF pilots and formed them to be used in Special Forces. They mainly worked with the French or for the French, but it was mainly working for SOE. If they had the right aircraft to pick them up, they

[1] Michael Richard Daniell Foot, CBE, TD, British Military Historian, former British Army Intelligence officer and special operation executive.

would take back agents in danger or who had some special information to give. They had to get it absolutely right or they could be landing in the middle of a forest. If they were landing some of the special forces, for example, there was the Lysander; it was ideal for landing people who could not for one reason or another be dropped by parachute, they might be carrying a very delicate cargo and they usually used a Lysander to carry the wireless.

"Most of the time they had the weather against them, and sometimes they could end up landing anywhere close to the chosen spot, so there was a big chance factor, and the same thing with people who were parachuted down from the Halifax planes. They used to call them "the drops". From 1944 to 1945 the Americans were also doing it, because they had big planes. They had to say in a certain phrase that they would drop so many men, or so many bits of equipment, ammunition or something, and then they had to alert the people who were going to receive them and they had to do it very carefully, because not only could *we* read the code, sometimes the Germans were very clever with their codes, too, and they did the same thing, so it was a rush as to who would get the code right; of course we had Bletchley Park to decipher. They also had to know a lot about the area, because the planes often had to come in very low. Flying by night to France had become more or less an art in the special forces or the RAF and they did it by following things like the light; they had to fly on moonlit nights, they used to call them "moon flights" because they had to have the light of the moon to help them work their route out. It took the best skilled pilots to be able to cope and normally the planes were small. The Lysander [2] was mainly for actual landings. If the plane was meant to come down in a nominated area, where the Resistance might be watching for them. They could also land in an area so dark it would be difficult to know where they were and there were a lot of groups caught because nobody knew where they were – nobody picked them up. Then, of course, you had the Halifax which, like the little Lysander, could land on

very small areas of land – some called it a little pocket handkerchief – and they could easily take off; it was usually to land and take off agents.

"They had a number of people going back and forth, you also had to realise the people who did it were new, perhaps they did not quite realise what was at stake. All the women who took part had to leave lives behind them. Before they went, they took different bits of equipment, one was the "suicide" pill, which was poison, and to my knowledge none of the women took it with them – they refused – although one or two were very sorry afterwards that they had. If you were captured you did not expect to survive and a lot of them ended up in a concentration camp, if they were not actually shot. In the concentration camp there was the gas chamber. They knew what they were doing, but it was also the spirit of adventure that motivated them and, of course, if something went wrong, they knew what they were taking on, they were told, "Are you sure, because you know, you might die?" They knew, it was drummed into them. Some had children, quite young children.

Most of them were captured and one or two or three escaped, but not very often. It was even worse for the resistance members who had helped them, and in many cases especially for their family, because if they were found out, they knew which village they came from and to which family they belonged. Only eight of the thirty-nine women in SOE France survived (there were only thirty-nine that I had got on my record who formed the SOE women). There were many more men, but I only wrote about the women. Most of my records said about four hundred went out, with thirty-nine women trained by SOE. Some of them who had gone to France, their role was to be keepers of safe houses, and the others were on the escape lines. There were some others, but not trained as SOE to do sabotage; they were there to get people out, technically speaking. But you see there were others, not just the ones mentioned in my book. Those in London, there were a lot, were also from different parts of Europe as well. Section F was for France, they also had groups from Belgium and Holland who had a very bad time because they were captured almost every time."

[2] The Lysander was a British army co-operation and liaison aircraft, the aircraft's exceptional short-filed performance enabled clandestine missions using small, unprepared airstrips behind enemy lines to place or recover agents, particularly in occupied France with the help of the French Resistance.

You wrote a lot of books about the WAAFs; what made you write them?

"Mainly because there was not much of a historical account. I wanted to recount their lives and what they did in the Second World War, there were one or two books already. I wanted to write about the women who went in the services, why they went into the WAAF, because they were known as the Women's Auxiliary Air Force then. The FANY were used as cover to be trained as SOE; nobody knew they were going in the SOE, they were being trained in properties belonging to FANY and they were all listed as FANY. The WAAF made them part of a regular service after the war, for their contribution during the war effort, which made them realise that they could not have succeeded without them. It was talked about in Parliament, in about 1943, as to what was going to happen to the women in the services, not just the RAF but also the army and navy.

After the war they did not have much money and they thought the women had to be demobbed, but then some wiser heads said, "Well, they have done some very good work and some of it was better done by women than men. Consequently they said there ought to be a small group that was kept on that were made regulars. They were on similar terms to the men, but only on two-thirds of the pay … well, they could not afford it, and in fact it was something of an achievement that they got allowed to become regular. My first book, *Women in Air Force Blue,* has lots of appendices; there were two editions. By the way, *Mission Improbable* is about the fifteen girls from the RAF who were part of the SOE. The RAF was very proud of them; out of thirty-nine they had fifteen, that was quite an achievement."

Did you have access to the archives?

I went to the archives of the army a bit, and the navy, and of course to the RAF ones that they kept moving. Then the Imperial War Museum (IWM) was very helpful, they gave me a launch in the IWM, all the senior officers that had been in the war came and had bought a book, and there were photographs in the press."

Books by Beryl Escott

Women in Air Force Blue: The story of women in the Royal Air Force from 1918 to the present day. Stephens, 1989.

Mission Improbable: A salute to RAF women of SOE in wartime France. Stevens (1991)

Our Wartime Days: The WAAF in World War II. A. Sutton (1995)

Twentieth Century Women of Courage. A. Sutton (1999)

WAAF. Osprey Publishing (2008)

The Heroines of SOE. Shire Publishing (2011)

DOROTHY WALLIS

Special Intelligence Officer, WAAF, 1941-1946

Dorothy lived in an immaculate flat in Shaftesbury. We met for first time near the town's war memorial and she very kindly followed all my instructions to pose in the photograph. It was only when we came back to her flat that she told me she could hardly see and was registered as blind.

Dorothy joined the WAAF in 1941. She was married at the time and her husband was also in the RAF. She was recruited after a stiff interview in German; she only had a rough idea but managed to get through the selection. Her parents were rather neutral about seeing their daughter joining the services. She was positioned in Yorkshire from 1943-45 on a Bomber Squadron base which had four groups of Halifax squadrons, after starting with some square-bashing in Brize Norton. She did a bit of everything in her role.

"There were usually three on duty. I was to be on twenty-four hour duty watch under special intelligence duties with the aircrew; I received the battle orders from headquarters and would tell each section the jobs they would have to do." Her job was quite secret and they were "asked to keep our mouths shut," as she put it; she hardly had any training and mostly learned on the job. They were pretty free to wear the jewellery they wanted during service hours as long as it did not show, and they were advised to wear their pearls otherwise they might lose their lustre. There were about a hundred women on the base, billeted in the woods. They sometimes ended up sharing a meal with some of the bomber squadron crew, knowing that they would be called on a mission the same evening; they could not tell them and would feel quite anxious for them.

Dorothy's marriage ended during the war. She stayed in service until the beginning of 1946, and after the war she went from the RAF to BOAC and became an Air Traffic Control assistant in Bournemouth (women could only be assistants) and remarried after ten years.

Dorothy used to love travelling; when I met her in the summer of 2011, she planned to go on a cruise in the Black Sea. Her son, John Wallis, got in touch with me after finding my letter to Dorothy requesting some pictures of her in uniform and agreed to send me these very treasured pictures.

Dorothy sadly passed away in the summer of 2012.

A photograph of Dorothy (unidentified) with her WAAF colleagues

ANGELA MARIA FRAMPTON

ATS, 1942-1946, posted in Italy at the Allied
Forces Headquarters

Angela Maria is ninety-three and lives in Northumberland, but when I met her she was on holiday at her daughter's house in Somerset. I came across Angela via her other daughter, Colette, who has written a book, *Women in the Second World War* (2011). She very kindly suggested that her mum would be happy to meet me.

Angela was a volunteer in the ATS between 1942 and 1946. When she joined there was a shortage of women, as "the officers' salaries had to be paid". Her dad was not happy at all about her choice but for her mum this was an advancement for women. Angela chose to join the ATS as they were desperate for women after the Dunkirk landings. She was part of the Southern Irish volunteers, who were also called the "Green Tab Ladies". Her first assignment was square-bashing for three months; she shared billets with girls from Scotland and Wales. She served two years in Helen's Bay outside Belfast in a beautiful place on the coast of Northern Ireland, before volunteering to go abroad. In the early mornings among the small boats they would spot a massive Red Cross ship, full of wounded and coming in to find a place in the hospital, outside Belfast. There were special places for them.

"My friend and I used to go into the hospitals in Belfast, we went where the pilots who lost their sight were, we used to go to write their letters," she told me. She was doing admin work but got "itchy feet" and was looking to go abroad. In late 1942, there was a call for people to go abroad, because men were going further up to the front; she volunteered and was sent to Italy (she had learned Italian at school) in 1943 and got a job at the Allied Forces Headquarters (FHQ) British team. The team was responsible for intelligence and security and Angela Maria was sworn to secrecy. They were based in Caserta, at the Royal Palace outside Naples, and only officers worked there.

Why did you choose the ATS?

"I was reading a paper, I think, and there was a call out for young women to join because they were getting scarce, quite a lot of Southern Irish girls chose to join and they gave us a green tab on our shoulder to show that we were Irish, the 'green tab ladies'. There were quite a few women, maybe 120. There were some Scottish as well as Welsh girls.

"Our uniform was a skirt and a little jacket with three-quarter sleeves, single breasted, with a little pocket. The girls in the WRNS had such a lovely uniform, you are never satisfied when you are young! We were not given a choice when I joined, I can't really remember, I think we did some sitting down to pass an exam. There were history and maths questions.

"I was chosen as office clerk and sent to the headquarters. I did admin, answered the phone, then I was starting to get itchy feet when they were calling for girls to go abroad, so I volunteered and was chosen; as I was working at the office they had a good idea about what my talents were. I was sent to London and we were put up in these houses in blocks with people, already living in them. There were people living in the middle ones but we never saw them; we had lectures and were shown all the museums.

"It was like a holiday, but we were actually waiting for the day we would be called to go abroad with the convoy. We went on a ship, a cruise liner transformed for troops. We went round via Malta, were on the boat three weeks and we saw all sorts of things, like flying fish. We ended up in Naples, and taken off and divided up. Then I was sent to Caserta Palace, three of us went there. There were ninety-six girls in a hangar all with different talents and jobs, and also linguists. I did clerical work with British Intelligence; that's all that I can I give you, I am sorry, but you can put down Intelligence."

So you spoke some Italian?

"Yes, I did, when I was at school there was a choice between German, French and Italian, and I took Italian. 'Isn't that weird?' my mother said. When I was at school I was learning French and I just could not learn it, I was crying over my lessons and my mum suggested I learn some Italian, because as a Catholic family we knew a lot of Latin. My mum used to say, "Whatever you are taught, if you like it or not, there will be a time in your life where you will need it." It is a lovely language, very melodious, the people were lovely. Where I worked there were all sorts of nationalities, we had Czechs and Polish girls and the languages they were all chattering in. These came directly from their own countries and we had a couple of Jewish and Palestinian girls, too."

Do you have any special anecdotes?

"I went to Monte Cassino, there was an American sergeant and me. They used to send intelligence people after the bombings to check if it really had happened, to verify it, and of course we were there that day. Walking to the top, what we saw was a landscape of desolation, the plain was transformed and the massive bomb craters were filled up with water and the monastery was nothing more than a hill of stones. There were still Polish soldiers there, as we got up near the top, picking up their fallen. When we were at the top, it was all battered, the road just falling away, it was just a field of old rocks.

"We could see a light flashing on a corner somewhere, so we all landed on the ground thinking some of the Germans were still up there flashing a signal down. We stayed down for some time until someone said, "It looks like it's a bloody wardrobe in the corner of a house with the door open and the mirror just catching in the wind," and it was true! It was just a corner left in a house and the wardrobe was in the corner. It was swinging back and forth.

"Where I was sitting, I saw everyone coming and going. When someone important was coming, the Royal Military Police (RMPs) the ones with the red caps on their heads, would come in. We were thinking, who is this with them? Right along the palace at the top, there were pools, big pools, and one of these was the officers' swimming pool and we used to be a little group up there. I got really badly burned. There were three diving boards up there with different heights, it was very nice. I met Jack there [her husband]. They came back from a raid and they were resting, and we used to go up there for swimming when I was off duty. It is amazing the people you meet in that situation that I would never have met in a lifetime. Amazing! Famous people even; I can't remember his name, but one was the future Earl of Harewood, cousin of the Queen.

"I was taken onto the desk to check identification when people wanted passes. They had to give all their stuff, information, and it was up to me if they could come or not. He was a colonel and he came in a fuss just around lunchtime. 'Where do you want to go?' I said. You don't question people like that, you just give them a pass when you are just a little squid.

"One day sitting in my office I overheard a lot of noise and it scared me, thinking that the Germans were coming back to my HQ; the last thing I was thinking was that they were coming to sign their rendition. History was being made at that very moment, it became all the more important with time.

"When I was there I met an aeroplane pilot and eventually we married out there at the Chapel Palace in 1945. The Home Office sent three bridal boxes with everything in, from bras to panties, with three different dresses; you had a choice. Mine was gorgeous, it was all beaded, it was so heavy. I bought some white satin shoes. I saved up all my chocolate, it must have been up to two pounds, to buy these lovely shoes I had seen in a small shop; they gave me the shoes for the chocolate. I had a lovely wedding there. When we came out of the Chapel, you had this big marble staircase. All the heads came along, all the American soldiers were standing alongside the British soldiers.

"The British chef in the canteen made a three-tier wedding cake, a beautiful wedding cake; we sent the small top back to the cookhouse and ate the middle, and cut all the other part up to share among Jack's crew and my friends. There was a bloody big hole in the roof following a bombing three weeks before the wedding and the wind was blowing with bits of dirt. We spent our honeymoon in Rome. The army had to find us a flat to stay in and provide security in that flat, because things were not all settled. We stayed with a lovely family, she was very good to me, a nice lady. After our meals in the mess we could go home to our flat. I left in 1946, late September, a year after I got married."

After the war Angela and her family were posted to the Suez Canal, where her husband was a fire and safety officer. They were hit by the Suez crisis in 1956 (the French and Israelis took the canal from Nasser) and had a road to hell travelling back to the UK.

How did your family react to you joining up?

"My father wasn't very happy, he thought everything was going to be bullets and bombing; my mother did not mind, she was a very forward-looking woman. She said, "If that's what you want." I understand my father coming from a little town in Ireland, wondering 'what's going to happen to her'. I just imagine myself, if I had one of my girls going. You've got to have a child to truly understand, I guess."

What would you say was your best experience joining as a volunteer?

"It was all very exciting, there were always nice people coming to that office as well, in Italy. I was in the Allied Headquarters at the Palace, there were all sorts of people coming, even General Montgomery came through one day, and they also brought some German officers through that were taken as prisoners."

Have you stayed in touch with other women over there?

"Nearly all of them are dead. I am ninety-three, I seem to be the only one that keeps hanging around."

Angela received five medals for her time in the services and overseas service.

SOE WOMEN AGENTS

Executed at Natzweiler-Struthof (France)

When I was a child I loved going to the Vosges mountains, I used to go skiing at the Champ-du-Feu with a school group every Wednesday. But the beautiful landscape over the Valley of Schirmeck also become a place of despair when Alsace was annexed by Germany in 1940 as they choose the nearby village of Natzweiler to build a concentration camp. I went to visit the camp (the only one on French soil) when I was at High School and found the experience quite daunting. My grandmother had already told me about how scared she was for her and her family to be sent there; she even told me that they could see the chimney of the crematorium burning from afar. Walking on the ground and realising what "*Nacht und Nebel*" really meant made it even more real.

While working on this project I decided to go back to revisit the camp. The gas chambers and the crematorium were closed to the public because of much-needed maintenance work. Passing through the heavy wooden doors and entering the camp still made me feel edgy. It was in the museum where I found a dedicated board to the four SOE agents who were secretly executed at the camp.

This camp was only for male prisoners, but in the summer of 1944 a group of well-dressed women were marched into the camp.

These women were:

Andrée Borrel (code name Denise), born in France and killed on July 6th, 1944, aged 25.

Vera Leigh (code name Simone), born in England and killed on July 6th, 1944, aged 41.

Sonia Olschanezky (code name Suzanne), born in Germany and killed on July 6th, 1944, aged 21.

Diana Rowden (code name Paulette), born in England and killed on July 6th, 1944, aged 29.

All the women had been arrested by the Gestapo and transferred from Fresnes Prison (near Paris). They had all joined the ranks of section F at the SOE as agents. Only Sonia had directly joined in France; the other women were parachuted in from the UK. In June 1942 Sonia was taken with 2000 other Jewish people, but her mother managed to convince a German official that she would be a key worker for the fur industry in Germany and bought her freedom, only for Sonia to join the Prosper network in 1943 and be betrayed, along with other agents, in January 1944.

The Struthof–Natzweiler Cocentration Camp entrance door

The memorial of the deportation, built to honour all deportees

CONCLUSION

This book is the result of a long quest in pursuit of understanding. Since 2003 I have been researching personal stories from World War Two, with a focus on researching women's roles during the war and integrating this research into this photography project.

This book is not a document for research or scholarly purposes; it is more about relating personal stories and presenting portrait photography with an individual approach. I wish that I could have added more portraits and testimonials from women who joined the army nursing services, the FANY, NAAFI, the WRAC or the SOE.

It is unfortunate that I was not allowed to speak to ladies in one nursing home who had been part of the FANY. Being given the opportunity to ask them questions directly would have been greatly appreciated. I also got in touch with Dame Vera Lynn, the 'Forces' Sweetheart', but she felt too old to be photographed. The Queen, you may ask? She joined as a volunteer in the ATS in 1945; I did not feel brave enough to write to her but I would more than welcome the opportunity to add her portrait and testimonial.

The women featured in this book and many others too did much behind the scenes, without much in the way of recognition. As Joy Lofthouse mentioned, the women who worked in munition factories never got the opportunity to walk down the march of fame for which other services had been praised. Formal recognition came late; the memorial dedicated to the Women of World War Two in Whitehall, London, was only erected in 2005.

I hope that you enjoy reading these personal stories, seeing the portraits and accompanying. These women are some of the last ones alive to speak about their wartime experiences in their own words, and I feel very privileged to have met them.

If you want to get in touch, please contact me at rachel@rachelvogeleisen.com or write to:

Dpt 140
30 Red Lion Street
TW9 1RB Richmond UK

ND - #0175 - 270225 - C88 - 254/203/7 - PB - 9781861513946 - Matt Lamination